CLASS
Lesson Planner

Christian Liberty Press

Arlington Heights, Illinois

A publication of

Christian Liberty Press

502 West Euclid Avenue

Arlington Heights, Illinois 60004

www.christianlibertypress.com

Created by Michael J. McHugh and Lina F. King

Layout and Editing by Edward J. Shewan

Copyediting by Diane C. Olson

Cover Design by Bob Fine

ISBN 978-1-930092-13-6
1-930092-13-X

Printed in the United States of America

Table of Contents

Introduction

Educating children often demands considerable time and effort. Few teachers can afford to waste time, and no educational program benefits from chaos or confusion. As in any endeavor, good organizational strategies and good tools often make the difference between success and failure.

The *CLASS Lesson Planner* has been designed by the staff of Christian Liberty Press to help home educators properly organize and manage their educational activities. Although some of the forms or strategies that are listed in this *Planner* will not be ideally suited to every home school, we are confident that most of the material will be of considerable help.

We encourage each instructor to start by reading the opening sections of the *Planner* that talk about general and specific organizational strategies as well as lesson plans. After reading this material, instructors will be better prepared to comprehend and fill out the yearly and weekly schedules that are included in the *Lesson Planner*. Based upon the assumption that most home schools will teach around 40 weeks each school term, we have provided 40 copies of the "Weekly Lesson Planner" form.

The last major section of the *CLASS Lesson Planner* includes various forms that will help teachers to manage their educational and family responsibilities. Some of these forms, such as the attendance form, should be filled out on a weekly basis. However, many of the forms—such as the report card, health, or transcript forms—are designed to be filled out on a quarterly or yearly basis. At the beginning of the school year, instructors should familiarize themselves with all the forms that have been provided to determine *which* forms they may wish to use during the year. This process will also permit instructors to decide *when* they will need to use them.

Parent-teachers should not feel pressured or compelled to use each and every form in the *CLASS Lesson Planner*. You and your students will profit from good planning and record keeping, but there is no need to let the *Lesson Planner* control your school. You need to commit yourself only to using those forms that truly benefit your educational program.

The Publishers

General Organization of Your Home School

Initially, planning a full year of school work for your children may seem to be a formidable task. However, by dividing your schedule into smaller units you will be able to more readily adapt to meet your personal needs. This is best done one step at a time.

Start by organizing your student's books (texts, workbooks, etc.), teacher support materials (answer keys, teacher's manuals, etc.), and testing materials (test packets, quizzes, etc.) to assure that you have everything needed for your student. List each text or workbook in a column; then, in the next column, write down the number of pages in each of them. In a third column, list the number of tests, quizzes, or drills to be used with each book. Watch for tests that may be printed and bound into a text or workbook.

With this basic data in front of you, you are now ready to start making decisions. How long do you want the school year to last? This is YOUR decision! You may decide to hold classes for only thirty-six weeks, or 180 days, as some states require. However, based on a forty-week school year, the twelve months would divide as follows:

Full Year			52 weeks
Less:	Summer vacation	8 weeks	
	Christmas break	1 week	
	Easter/Spring break	1 week	
	Ten Holidays, sick days	<u>2 weeks</u>	
		12 weeks ➠	<u>-12 weeks</u>
Remaining weeks for YOUR school year			40 weeks

Next, divide the number of pages in each book by forty, minus any weeks set aside for review and testing. This will give you an approximate weekly goal for each book.

Some books can be completed in less than forty weeks. This leads to various ways of dividing up the school year. *First*, you may plan on completing each of your books in thirty to forty weeks. If any are done in less than forty weeks, then the time previously spent on them can be used for other subjects during the last few weeks of your forty-week schedule. *Second*, you may plan on completing some books in one half (or some other fraction) of the year; then, the rest of the year, you may use their time slots for   different books. However, most home school families will benefit from providing an even balance of course work over the entire school term.

Third, dividing 180 to 200 school days into the pages of a textbook is an alternate method for determining the amount of work that should be completed each day. Also remember to set aside days for review and testing.

Kindergarten children will normally be in academic studies for just the morning hours. In most cases, it is counter-productive to push kindergarten children to study academic subjects for more than three or four hours per day.

We suggest that a normal school day with standard vacation periods throughout the year be followed. Many home schoolers follow the attendance schedule of a local Christian day school.

In addition, students should study in a quiet place. Develop a "school room" atmosphere. Avoid the use of TV during school hours, unless you are presenting an educational video.

Concerts, museum visits, and other field trip activities should be scheduled. We also encourage participation in extra-curricular programs, church activities, clubs, choirs, and community activities such as 4-H clubs and sports programs. A special form is provided with this *Planner* that helps you to schedule field trip activities.

Two Forms of Scheduling

Traditional Day-School Schedule:

8:30	–	9:15	Mathematics
9:15	–	10:00	Reading
10:00	–	10:45	Science
10:45	–	11:30	History/Geography
11:30	–	12:15	Lunch
12:15	–	1:00	Bible
1:00	–	1:45	Grammar/Handwriting
1:45	–	2:30	Art/Music
2:30	–	3:15	Physical Education

Most of you are familiar with *traditional day-school schedules* and their rigid time slots punctuated by bells. In making up their own schedule, most people attempt to follow a pattern similar to the "Traditional Day-School Schedule" as listed above. While this rigid, structured schedule may look nice on paper, *it just does not work for most home schools.* This brings us to one of the great advantages of homeschooling. Because you are not really bound by rigid schedules and bells ringing every forty-five minutes, you can truly adapt your program to fit the needs of your student(s) and your own needs. After considering your student's age, attention span, abilities, and possible educational deficiencies, you may find that a *modified traditional schedule* may better serve your needs and prove to be a more realistic structure for achieving your goals.

Distinguishing Features of Each Form of Scheduling

First form of scheduling – Traditional

1. Rigid periods that contain the identical length of time

2. Courses scheduled in the same time frame each day

3. All required courses taught each day (art and music, however, may be taught various times a week)

Second form of scheduling – Modified Traditional

1. Periods are more flexible, allowing for adjustable time frames that expand or contract as educational needs dictate. For example, if a math lesson is finished in thirty minutes, the student may go immediately to the next course of study or take time for a break.

2. Subjects are still scheduled each day at approximately the same time. However, flexibility allows for different starting and stopping times when necessary. Difficult courses will sometimes require longer periods of time; less demanding subjects may require shorter periods of time.

3. All courses are taught each day (art, music, and physical education through the week as scheduled).

We would not encourage you to schedule one subject per day; that is, trying to cram an entire week's work into one day. Difficult subjects, such as math and grammar, are best mastered by studying a portion every day. In this way, one lesson or concept can be studied per day. The repetition of the exercises and drill work aid in understanding and are a necessary part of that day's lesson.

To cram a week's worth of lessons into one day is like a man who eats all day one day per week in an attempt to take care of all his nutritional needs for the week. We can see the folly of this, and the same principle holds true with learning. We need time to digest and assimilate facts so that they become true knowledge.

Tackle Difficult Subjects First

Difficult subjects should not be put off until last. Psychologically, it is better to attack the difficult subjects first while you are still fresh. It is a real boost to know that "Mount Everest" is behind you, and the remainder of the day can be devoted to the more enjoyable, less demanding subjects.

Stagger Your Difficult Courses

With multiple students, flexibility within a schedule is even more important. We suggest you "stagger" the difficult subjects so that the one-on-one attention can be given as needed. While this tends to make greater demands on the mother (who is usually the teacher), she can manage her daily teaching schedule better if she keeps in mind the need to schedule the difficult subjects for one child while another tends to reading and independent study of a more routine nature.

Making the Transition

The transition into home education can be quite nerve-racking for the simple reason that parent-teachers are often inexperienced in teaching; and, consequently, find it difficult to organize themselves because they are without a model or example to follow.

The failure of many home schoolers can often be traced to organizational patterns that are both inconsistent and extreme in approach. A popular organizational pitfall is the attempt by parents to organize their home school exactly like the traditional Christian school. In a relatively short period of time, parent and students alike find it impossible to turn their home school environment into a traditional school and succumb to the phenomenon known as "home school burnout."

Unfortunately, many home school parents overreact to this problem and, in their frustration, decide to do away with structure altogether. The result of this experiment in extremes is loss of time, wheel spinning, and general confusion as students start to fall behind and flounder in their studies. A significant number of families do not survive their first year in home education because they feel they have failed in the task of establishing a reasonable school schedule.

In conclusion, home teachers must learn to relax and provide themselves with a realistic amount of transition time. Very few home school families hold to the *exact* same schedule. The long-range goal of instructors should be to fall into a structured learning pattern that is flexible enough to promote both *self-discipline* and *personal achievement*. In short, planning your work and working your plan must go hand-in-hand with adaptability and flexibility. It is a delicate balance, but it can be achieved.

Your plan is the means to an end, not an end in itself. For many, a personally modified traditional schedule is a more realistic means to achieve a successful and enjoyable home school program.

Lesson Planning Instructions

Your daily lesson plan should consist of the following three components:

First: Review old material. Never proceed to the presentation of new material if the student has not demonstrated an understanding of previous material presented. Old material must be understood before proceeding to the next step.

Second: Present new material. When you are assured that the student has sufficiently understood the directions to work independently, assign material for the day.

Third: Verify the student's understanding. Check the completed school work before the student finishes the day's lesson. If the student still does not understand, this is the time to explain the material once again. Also, the teacher has the option, depending on what serves your needs best, to either check the "homework" assignment later that day, or during the review period of the next lesson.

Outline of Teacher's Lesson Plan

I. Review

   1. Discuss the important points from the previous day's lesson.

   2. Use flashcards or drill problems where appropriate.

   3. Correct homework together, and re-work any materials not understood before introducing new materials.

II. Introduce New Materials

   1. Read the directions carefully to the student, or have the student read these aloud. Thoroughly explain all directions or processes before beginning. Be sure to clearly establish goals for the student to reach.

   2. Assign classwork. Work not completed during class time may be assigned as "homework."

III. Verify Understanding of New Material

   1. Quickly scan the student's work to determine if the student understands the day's lesson. Provide an oral quiz whenever possible.

   2. Point out errors. Repeat the explanation, if necessary, to assure the student understands the material and has achieved the specific academic goals that were set forth at the beginning of the lesson.

Yearly School Calendar

Home educators, as well as traditional private schools, can benefit from a school calendar that draws attention to important events or activities that are planned for the student body. Without such a listing, educators are often prone to become so focused on the day-to-day activities of teaching that they lose the "big picture" of their yearly goals. In addition, a school calendar can function as a type of "bulletin board" which reminds busy teachers or parents of their long and short range plans.

We suggest that you note the basic plans and activities of the school year at the beginning of the school term, with the understanding that you will need to modify or expand upon your basic plans as the school year progresses. Please note the sample monthly schedule for December.

DECEMBER				YEAR 20 _____
Monday	**Tuesday**	**Wednesday**	**Thursday**	**Friday**
			1 Listen to Algebra Video	2
5 Science fair at Church Gym 6 pm	6	7 Choir practice for Girls 4 pm	8	9 Complete Progress Report
12 Phone Congress regarding H.S. Legislation	13	14 Choir practice for Girls 4 pm	15	16 Gymnastics Class at YMCA 3:45 pm
19 Christmas Break	20 Christmas Break	21 Christmas Break	22 Christmas Break	23 Christmas Break
26 Field Trip to County Zoo	27	28 Choir practice for Girls 4 pm	29	30 Gymnastics Class at YMCA 3:45 pm

September

Year 20 _____

Monday	Tuesday	Wednesday	Thursday	Friday

October

Year 20 _____

Monday	Tuesday	Wednesday	Thursday	Friday

November

YEAR 20 _____

Monday	Tuesday	Wednesday	Thursday	Friday

December

YEAR 20 _____

Monday	Tuesday	Wednesday	Thursday	Friday

JANUARY

Monday	Tuesday	Wednesday	Thursday	Friday

FEBRUARY

Monday	Tuesday	Wednesday	Thursday	Friday

MARCH				YEAR 20 _____
Monday	Tuesday	Wednesday	Thursday	Friday

APRIL				YEAR 20 _____
Monday	Tuesday	Wednesday	Thursday	Friday

MAY				YEAR 20 _____
Monday	Tuesday	Wednesday	Thursday	Friday

JUNE				YEAR 20 _____
Monday	Tuesday	Wednesday	Thursday	Friday

JULY				YEAR 20 _____
Monday	**Tuesday**	**Wednesday**	**Thursday**	**Friday**

AUGUST				YEAR 20 _____
Monday	**Tuesday**	**Wednesday**	**Thursday**	**Friday**

Weekly

Lesson Plan

Forms

Student: _John Smith_   Grade: _4_   Week Beginning: _Sept. 5_

Weekly Lesson Planner

Day	Bible	Quiz or Test	Main Concepts to Cover	Date Covered
Mon	Complete pages 1–3		The Days of Creation	9/5
Tues	Complete pages 4–6 and give quiz	Quiz	The Meaning of Genesis	9/6
Wed	Complete pages 7–10		The Purpose for Creation	9/7
Thur	Complete pages 11–14		The Fall of Adam and Eve	9/8
Fri	Review Chapter 1	Test	Give an overview of Genesis	9/9

Specific concepts that still need to be reviewed/re-emphasized: _Review the days of creation and the plan of salvation through a promised Redeemer._   Date Review Completed: _9 / 12 / 2010_

Day	Reading	Quiz or Test	Main Concepts to Cover	Date Covered
Mon	Read: The Story of the Robin pp. 1–3		Vocabulary and pronunciation skills	9/5
Tues	Read: The Story of the Robin pp. 4–6	Oral Quiz	Reading speed and comprehension	9/6
Wed	Read: The Call of Mrs. White pp. 7–10		Vocabulary and leading characters	9/7
Thur	Read: The Call of Mrs. White pp. 11–14	Oral Quiz	Style of author and mood or tone	9/8
Fri	Review the two reading selections		Discuss the moral of the stories	9/9

Specific concepts that still need to be reviewed/re-emphasized: _Review phonics fundamentals to improve pronunciation skills and talk about the main plot of the stories._   Date Review Completed: _9 / 12 / 2010_

Day	Spelling/Handwriting	Quiz or Test	Main Concepts to Cover	Date Covered
Mon	Spelling workbook–Unit 1, Lesson 1		Handling prefixes and suffixes	9/5
Tues	Handwriting book pages 1–2		Letter formation and spacing	9/6
Wed	Spelling workbook–Unit 1, Lessons 2 – 3	Quiz	Practice weekly spelling list	9/7
Thur	Handwriting book pages 3-4		Practice with capital letters	9/8
Fri	Spelling workbook–Unit 1, Lessons 4 – 5	Unit Test	Word endings and final test	9/9

Specific concepts that still need to be reviewed/re-emphasized: _Student still needs to learn how to put the correct space between each letter. Review spelling test._   Date Review Completed: _9 / 12 / 2010_

Day	Grammar/Phonics	Quiz or Test	Main Concepts to Cover	Date Covered
Mon	Complete pages 1–3 in grammar		Study antonyms	9/5
Tues	Complete pages 4–6		Study synonyms	9/6
Wed	Complete pages 7–9 and give quiz	Oral Quiz	Study contractions	9/7
Thur	Complete pages 10–14		Study root words	9/8
Fri	Finish chapter one and give final test	Test	Study chapter concepts	9/9

Specific concepts that still need to be reviewed/re-emphasized: _Student needs more practice with contractions_   Date Review Completed: _9 / 12 / 2010_

Day	History	Quiz or Test	Main Concepts to Cover	Date Covered
Mon	Read pages 1–3		Life of Leif Ericson / Vikings	9/5
Tues	Read pages 4–6		Age of Exploration in overview	9/6
Wed	Read pages 7–9 and give quiz	Oral Quiz	Life and times of Columbus	9/7
Thur	Read pages 10–12		Native American Settlements	9/8
Fri	Review chapter and complete exercises	Chpt. Test	Early Trade Routes and Geography	9/9

Specific concepts that still need to be reviewed/re-emphasized: _The student needs to review a time line of early American history to better understand this time period._   Date Review Completed: _9 / 12 / 2010_

Day	Science	Quiz or Test	Main Concepts to Cover	Date Covered
Mon	Read pages 1–3		Principles of Observation	9/5
Tues	Read pages 4–6		Forming a hypothesis	9/6
Wed	Read pages 7–8 and give quiz	Oral Quiz	Testing a hypothesis	9/7
Thur	Read pp. 9–14 and perform experiments		Explanation of Spontaneous generation	9/8
Fri	Review chapter and finish exercises	Test	The Law of Biogenesis	9/9

Specific concepts that still need to be reviewed/re-emphasized: _Proper use for experimentation and its limits. Explain why scientific theories are often based on faith, not observation._   Date Review Completed: _9 / 12 / 2010_

Day	Math	Quiz or Test	Main Concepts to Cover	Date Covered
Mon	Complete pages 1–3		Double digit addition and subtraction	9/5
Tues	Complete pages 4–6 and give quiz	Oral Quiz	Multiply by 1, 2, or 3	9/6
Wed	Complete pages 7–10		Simple fractions	9/7
Thur	Complete pages 11–14		Triple-digit addition/subtraction	9/8
Fri	Complete the review exercises on page 15	Test	Simple division facts	9/9

Specific concepts that still need to be reviewed/re-emphasized: _More review is needed with triple-digit addition and subtraction_   Date Review Completed: _9 / 12 / 2010_

Day	_Geography_	Quiz or Test	Main Concepts to Cover	Date Covered
Mon	Read pages 1–3		Study land formations and oceans	9/5
Tues	Complete exercises on pages 4–5		Review of continents	9/6
Wed	Read pages 6–7		Introduction to charts and graphs	9/7
Thur	Complete exercises on pp. 8–9; give quiz	Oral Quiz	Geography of the Americas	9/8
Fri	Complete lesson review on page 10		Finding locations on the globe	9/9

Specific concepts that still need to be reviewed/re-emphasized: _Review the use of globe skills, especially longitude and latitude._   Date Review Completed: _9 / 12 / 2010_

Listing of Daily Work or Tests that will be sent to CLASS this week:

Item(s) Mailed: _____Chapter 1 Grammar test_____   Date: ___ _9 / 12 / 2010_

Item(s) Mailed: _____Chapter 1 History test_____   Date: ___ _9 / 12 / 2010_

Item(s) Mailed: _____Chapter 1 Science test_____   Date: ___ _9 / 12 / 2010_

Item(s) Mailed: _____Chapter 1 Math test_____   Date: ___ _9 / 12 / 2010_

Student: _____ Grade: _____ Week Beginning: _____

Weekly Lesson Planner

Day	Bible	Quiz or Test	Main Concepts to Cover	Date Covered
Mon				
Tues				
Wed				
Thur				
Fri				

Specific concepts that still need to be reviewed/re-emphasized: _____

_____ Date Review Completed: __/__/20__

Day	Reading	Quiz or Test	Main Concepts to Cover	Date Covered
Mon				
Tues				
Wed				
Thur				
Fri				

Specific concepts that still need to be reviewed/re-emphasized: _____

_____ Date Review Completed: __/__/20__

Day	Spelling and Handwriting	Quiz or Test	Main Concepts to Cover	Date Covered
Mon				
Tues				
Wed				
Thur				
Fri				

Specific concepts that still need to be reviewed/re-emphasized: _____

_____ Date Review Completed: __/__/20__

Day	Grammar and Phonics	Quiz or Test	Main Concepts to Cover	Date Covered
Mon				
Tues				
Wed				
Thur				
Fri				

Specific concepts that still need to be reviewed/re-emphasized: _____

_____ Date Review Completed: __/__/20__

Day	History	Quiz or Test	Main Concepts to Cover	Date Covered
Mon				
Tues				
Wed				
Thur				
Fri				

Specific concepts that still need to be reviewed/re-emphasized: _____

_____ Date Review Completed: __/__/20__

Day	Science	Quiz or Test	Main Concepts to Cover	Date Covered
Mon				
Tues				
Wed				
Thur				
Fri				

Specific concepts that still need to be reviewed/re-emphasized: _____

_____ Date Review Completed: __/__/20__

Day	Math	Quiz or Test	Main Concepts to Cover	Date Covered
Mon				
Tues				
Wed				
Thur				
Fri				

Specific concepts that still need to be reviewed/re-emphasized: _____

_____ Date Review Completed: __/__/20__

Day	Other: _____	Quiz or Test	Main Concepts to Cover	Date Covered
Mon				
Tues				
Wed				
Thur				
Fri				

Specific concepts that still need to be reviewed/re-emphasized: _____

_____ Date Review Completed: __/__/20__

General Comments: _____

_____

Student: _____ Grade: _____ Week Beginning: _____

Weekly Lesson Planner

Day	Bible	Quiz or Test	Main Concepts to Cover	Date Covered
Mon				
Tues				
Wed				
Thur				
Fri				

Specific concepts that still need to be reviewed/re-emphasized: _____

_____ Date Review Completed: __/__/20__

Day	Reading	Quiz or Test	Main Concepts to Cover	Date Covered
Mon				
Tues				
Wed				
Thur				
Fri				

Specific concepts that still need to be reviewed/re-emphasized: _____

_____ Date Review Completed: __/__/20__

Day	Spelling and Handwriting	Quiz or Test	Main Concepts to Cover	Date Covered
Mon				
Tues				
Wed				
Thur				
Fri				

Specific concepts that still need to be reviewed/re-emphasized: _____

_____ Date Review Completed: __/__/20__

Day	Grammar and Phonics	Quiz or Test	Main Concepts to Cover	Date Covered
Mon				
Tues				
Wed				
Thur				
Fri				

Specific concepts that still need to be reviewed/re-emphasized: _____

_____ Date Review Completed: __/__/20__

Day	History	Quiz or Test	Main Concepts to Cover	Date Covered
Mon				
Tues				
Wed				
Thur				
Fri				

Specific concepts that still need to be reviewed/re-emphasized: _____

_____ Date Review Completed: __/__/20__

Day	Science	Quiz or Test	Main Concepts to Cover	Date Covered
Mon				
Tues				
Wed				
Thur				
Fri				

Specific concepts that still need to be reviewed/re-emphasized: _____

_____ Date Review Completed: __/__/20__

Day	Math	Quiz or Test	Main Concepts to Cover	Date Covered
Mon				
Tues				
Wed				
Thur				
Fri				

Specific concepts that still need to be reviewed/re-emphasized: _____

_____ Date Review Completed: __/__/20__

Day	Other: _____	Quiz or Test	Main Concepts to Cover	Date Covered
Mon				
Tues				
Wed				
Thur				
Fri				

Specific concepts that still need to be reviewed/re-emphasized: _____

_____ Date Review Completed: __/__/20__

General Comments: _____

_____

Student: _____ Grade: _____ Week Beginning: _____

Weekly Lesson Planner

Day	Bible	Quiz or Test	Main Concepts to Cover	Date Covered
Mon				
Tues				
Wed				
Thur				
Fri				

Specific concepts that still need to be reviewed/re-emphasized: _____
_____ Date Review Completed: _/_/20__

Day	Reading	Quiz or Test	Main Concepts to Cover	Date Covered
Mon				
Tues				
Wed				
Thur				
Fri				

Specific concepts that still need to be reviewed/re-emphasized: _____
_____ Date Review Completed: _/_/20__

Day	Spelling and Handwriting	Quiz or Test	Main Concepts to Cover	Date Covered
Mon				
Tues				
Wed				
Thur				
Fri				

Specific concepts that still need to be reviewed/re-emphasized: _____
_____ Date Review Completed: _/_/20__

Day	Grammar and Phonics	Quiz or Test	Main Concepts to Cover	Date Covered
Mon				
Tues				
Wed				
Thur				
Fri				

Specific concepts that still need to be reviewed/re-emphasized: _____
_____ Date Review Completed: _/_/20__

Day	History	Quiz or Test	Main Concepts to Cover	Date Covered
Mon				
Tues				
Wed				
Thur				
Fri				

Specific concepts that still need to be reviewed/re-emphasized: _____
_____   Date Review Completed: __/__/20__

Day	Science	Quiz or Test	Main Concepts to Cover	Date Covered
Mon				
Tues				
Wed				
Thur				
Fri				

Specific concepts that still need to be reviewed/re-emphasized: _____
_____   Date Review Completed: __/__/20__

Day	Math	Quiz or Test	Main Concepts to Cover	Date Covered
Mon				
Tues				
Wed				
Thur				
Fri				

Specific concepts that still need to be reviewed/re-emphasized: _____
_____   Date Review Completed: __/__/20__

Day	Other: _____	Quiz or Test	Main Concepts to Cover	Date Covered
Mon				
Tues				
Wed				
Thur				
Fri				

Specific concepts that still need to be reviewed/re-emphasized: _____
_____   Date Review Completed: __/__/20__

General Comments: _____
_____

Student: _____   Grade: _____   Week Beginning: _____

Weekly Lesson Planner

Day	Bible	Quiz or Test	Main Concepts to Cover	Date Covered
Mon				
Tues				
Wed				
Thur				
Fri				

Specific concepts that still need to be reviewed/re-emphasized: _____

_____   Date Review Completed: __/__/20__

Day	Reading	Quiz or Test	Main Concepts to Cover	Date Covered
Mon				
Tues				
Wed				
Thur				
Fri				

Specific concepts that still need to be reviewed/re-emphasized: _____

_____   Date Review Completed: __/__/20__

Day	Spelling and Handwriting	Quiz or Test	Main Concepts to Cover	Date Covered
Mon				
Tues				
Wed				
Thur				
Fri				

Specific concepts that still need to be reviewed/re-emphasized: _____

_____   Date Review Completed: __/__/20__

Day	Grammar and Phonics	Quiz or Test	Main Concepts to Cover	Date Covered
Mon				
Tues				
Wed				
Thur				
Fri				

Specific concepts that still need to be reviewed/re-emphasized: _____

_____   Date Review Completed: __/__/20__

Day	History	Quiz or Test	Main Concepts to Cover	Date Covered
Mon				
Tues				
Wed				
Thur				
Fri				

Specific concepts that still need to be reviewed/re-emphasized: _____

_____ Date Review Completed: __/__/20__

Day	Science	Quiz or Test	Main Concepts to Cover	Date Covered
Mon				
Tues				
Wed				
Thur				
Fri				

Specific concepts that still need to be reviewed/re-emphasized: _____

_____ Date Review Completed: __/__/20__

Day	Math	Quiz or Test	Main Concepts to Cover	Date Covered
Mon				
Tues				
Wed				
Thur				
Fri				

Specific concepts that still need to be reviewed/re-emphasized: _____

_____ Date Review Completed: __/__/20__

Day	Other: _____	Quiz or Test	Main Concepts to Cover	Date Covered
Mon				
Tues				
Wed				
Thur				
Fri				

Specific concepts that still need to be reviewed/re-emphasized: _____

_____ Date Review Completed: __/__/20__

General Comments: _____

_____

Student: _____ Grade: _____ Week Beginning: _____

Weekly Lesson Planner

Day	Bible	Quiz or Test	Main Concepts to Cover	Date Covered
Mon				
Tues				
Wed				
Thur				
Fri				

Specific concepts that still need to be reviewed/re-emphasized: _____
_____ Date Review Completed: __/__/20__

Day	Reading	Quiz or Test	Main Concepts to Cover	Date Covered
Mon				
Tues				
Wed				
Thur				
Fri				

Specific concepts that still need to be reviewed/re-emphasized: _____
_____ Date Review Completed: __/__/20__

Day	Spelling and Handwriting	Quiz or Test	Main Concepts to Cover	Date Covered
Mon				
Tues				
Wed				
Thur				
Fri				

Specific concepts that still need to be reviewed/re-emphasized: _____
_____ Date Review Completed: __/__/20__

Day	Grammar and Phonics	Quiz or Test	Main Concepts to Cover	Date Covered
Mon				
Tues				
Wed				
Thur				
Fri				

Specific concepts that still need to be reviewed/re-emphasized: _____
_____ Date Review Completed: __/__/20__

Day	History	Quiz or Test	Main Concepts to Cover	Date Covered
Mon				
Tues				
Wed				
Thur				
Fri				

Specific concepts that still need to be reviewed/re-emphasized: _____
_____   Date Review Completed: __/__/20__

Day	Science	Quiz or Test	Main Concepts to Cover	Date Covered
Mon				
Tues				
Wed				
Thur				
Fri				

Specific concepts that still need to be reviewed/re-emphasized: _____
_____   Date Review Completed: __/__/20__

Day	Math	Quiz or Test	Main Concepts to Cover	Date Covered
Mon				
Tues				
Wed				
Thur				
Fri				

Specific concepts that still need to be reviewed/re-emphasized: _____
_____   Date Review Completed: __/__/20__

Day	Other: _____	Quiz or Test	Main Concepts to Cover	Date Covered
Mon				
Tues				
Wed				
Thur				
Fri				

Specific concepts that still need to be reviewed/re-emphasized: _____
_____   Date Review Completed: __/__/20__

General Comments: _____

_____

Student: _____ Grade: _____ Week Beginning: _____

Weekly Lesson Planner

Day	Bible	Quiz or Test	Main Concepts to Cover	Date Covered
Mon				
Tues				
Wed				
Thur				
Fri				

Specific concepts that still need to be reviewed/re-emphasized: _____

_____ Date Review Completed: __/__/20__

Day	Reading	Quiz or Test	Main Concepts to Cover	Date Covered
Mon				
Tues				
Wed				
Thur				
Fri				

Specific concepts that still need to be reviewed/re-emphasized: _____

_____ Date Review Completed: __/__/20__

Day	Spelling and Handwriting	Quiz or Test	Main Concepts to Cover	Date Covered
Mon				
Tues				
Wed				
Thur				
Fri				

Specific concepts that still need to be reviewed/re-emphasized: _____

_____ Date Review Completed: __/__/20__

Day	Grammar and Phonics	Quiz or Test	Main Concepts to Cover	Date Covered
Mon				
Tues				
Wed				
Thur				
Fri				

Specific concepts that still need to be reviewed/re-emphasized: _____

Date Review Completed: __/__/20__

Day	History	Quiz or Test	Main Concepts to Cover	Date Covered
Mon				
Tues				
Wed				
Thur				
Fri				

Specific concepts that still need to be reviewed/re-emphasized: _____

_____   Date Review Completed: __/__/20__

Day	Science	Quiz or Test	Main Concepts to Cover	Date Covered
Mon				
Tues				
Wed				
Thur				
Fri				

Specific concepts that still need to be reviewed/re-emphasized: _____

_____   Date Review Completed: __/__/20__

Day	Math	Quiz or Test	Main Concepts to Cover	Date Covered
Mon				
Tues				
Wed				
Thur				
Fri				

Specific concepts that still need to be reviewed/re-emphasized: _____

_____   Date Review Completed: __/__/20__

Day	Other: _____	Quiz or Test	Main Concepts to Cover	Date Covered
Mon				
Tues				
Wed				
Thur				
Fri				

Specific concepts that still need to be reviewed/re-emphasized: _____

_____   Date Review Completed: __/__/20__

General Comments: _____

_____

Student: _____ Grade: _____ Week Beginning: _____

Weekly Lesson Planner

Day	Bible	Quiz or Test	Main Concepts to Cover	Date Covered
Mon				
Tues				
Wed				
Thur				
Fri				

Specific concepts that still need to be reviewed/re-emphasized: _____

_____   Date Review Completed: __/ __/20__

Day	Reading	Quiz or Test	Main Concepts to Cover	Date Covered
Mon				
Tues				
Wed				
Thur				
Fri				

Specific concepts that still need to be reviewed/re-emphasized: _____

_____   Date Review Completed: __/ __/20__

Day	Spelling and Handwriting	Quiz or Test	Main Concepts to Cover	Date Covered
Mon				
Tues				
Wed				
Thur				
Fri				

Specific concepts that still need to be reviewed/re-emphasized: _____

_____   Date Review Completed: __/ __/20__

Day	Grammar and Phonics	Quiz or Test	Main Concepts to Cover	Date Covered
Mon				
Tues				
Wed				
Thur				
Fri				

Specific concepts that still need to be reviewed/re-emphasized: _____

_____   Date Review Completed: __/ __/20__

Day	History	Quiz or Test	Main Concepts to Cover	Date Covered
Mon				
Tues				
Wed				
Thur				
Fri				

Specific concepts that still need to be reviewed/re-emphasized: _____

_____ Date Review Completed: _/ _/ 20_

Day	Science	Quiz or Test	Main Concepts to Cover	Date Covered
Mon				
Tues				
Wed				
Thur				
Fri				

Specific concepts that still need to be reviewed/re-emphasized: _____

_____ Date Review Completed: _/ _/ 20_

Day	Math	Quiz or Test	Main Concepts to Cover	Date Covered
Mon				
Tues				
Wed				
Thur				
Fri				

Specific concepts that still need to be reviewed/re-emphasized: _____

_____ Date Review Completed: _/ _/ 20_

Day	Other: _____	Quiz or Test	Main Concepts to Cover	Date Covered
Mon				
Tues				
Wed				
Thur				
Fri				

Specific concepts that still need to be reviewed/re-emphasized: _____

_____ Date Review Completed: _/ _/ 20_

General Comments: _____

_____

Student: _____ Grade: _____ Week Beginning: _____

Weekly Lesson Planner

Day	Bible	Quiz or Test	Main Concepts to Cover	Date Covered
Mon				
Tues				
Wed				
Thur				
Fri				

Specific concepts that still need to be reviewed/re-emphasized: _____
_____ Date Review Completed: _/ / 20__

Day	Reading	Quiz or Test	Main Concepts to Cover	Date Covered
Mon				
Tues				
Wed				
Thur				
Fri				

Specific concepts that still need to be reviewed/re-emphasized: _____
_____ Date Review Completed: _/ / 20__

Day	Spelling and Handwriting	Quiz or Test	Main Concepts to Cover	Date Covered
Mon				
Tues				
Wed				
Thur				
Fri				

Specific concepts that still need to be reviewed/re-emphasized: _____
_____ Date Review Completed: _/ / 20__

Day	Grammar and Phonics	Quiz or Test	Main Concepts to Cover	Date Covered
Mon				
Tues				
Wed				
Thur				
Fri				

Specific concepts that still need to be reviewed/re-emphasized: _____
_____ Date Review Completed: _/ / 20__

Day	History	Quiz or Test	Main Concepts to Cover	Date Covered
Mon				
Tues				
Wed				
Thur				
Fri				

Specific concepts that still need to be reviewed/re-emphasized: _____

_____ Date Review Completed: __/__/20__

Day	Science	Quiz or Test	Main Concepts to Cover	Date Covered
Mon				
Tues				
Wed				
Thur				
Fri				

Specific concepts that still need to be reviewed/re-emphasized: _____

_____ Date Review Completed: __/__/20__

Day	Math	Quiz or Test	Main Concepts to Cover	Date Covered
Mon				
Tues				
Wed				
Thur				
Fri				

Specific concepts that still need to be reviewed/re-emphasized: _____

_____ Date Review Completed: __/__/20__

Day	Other: _____	Quiz or Test	Main Concepts to Cover	Date Covered
Mon				
Tues				
Wed				
Thur				
Fri				

Specific concepts that still need to be reviewed/re-emphasized: _____

_____ Date Review Completed: __/__/20__

General Comments: _____

_____

Student: _____ Grade: _____ Week Beginning: _____

Weekly Lesson Planner

Day	Bible	Quiz or Test	Main Concepts to Cover	Date Covered
Mon				
Tues				
Wed				
Thur				
Fri				

Specific concepts that still need to be reviewed/re-emphasized: _____

_____

Date Review Completed: __ / __ / 20 __

Day	Reading	Quiz or Test	Main Concepts to Cover	Date Covered
Mon				
Tues				
Wed				
Thur				
Fri				

Specific concepts that still need to be reviewed/re-emphasized: _____

_____

Date Review Completed: __ / __ / 20 __

Day	Spelling and Handwriting	Quiz or Test	Main Concepts to Cover	Date Covered
Mon				
Tues				
Wed				
Thur				
Fri				

Specific concepts that still need to be reviewed/re-emphasized: _____

_____

Date Review Completed: __ / __ / 20 __

Day	Grammar and Phonics	Quiz or Test	Main Concepts to Cover	Date Covered
Mon				
Tues				
Wed				
Thur				
Fri				

Specific concepts that still need to be reviewed/re-emphasized: _____

_____

Date Review Completed: __ / __ / 20 __

Day	History	Quiz or Test	Main Concepts to Cover	Date Covered
Mon				
Tues				
Wed				
Thur				
Fri				

Specific concepts that still need to be reviewed/re-emphasized: _____

_____   Date Review Completed: ___/__/20___

Day	Science	Quiz or Test	Main Concepts to Cover	Date Covered
Mon				
Tues				
Wed				
Thur				
Fri				

Specific concepts that still need to be reviewed/re-emphasized: _____

_____   Date Review Completed: ___/__/20___

Day	Math	Quiz or Test	Main Concepts to Cover	Date Covered
Mon				
Tues				
Wed				
Thur				
Fri				

Specific concepts that still need to be reviewed/re-emphasized: _____

_____   Date Review Completed: ___/__/20___

Day	Other: _____	Quiz or Test	Main Concepts to Cover	Date Covered
Mon				
Tues				
Wed				
Thur				
Fri				

Specific concepts that still need to be reviewed/re-emphasized: _____

_____   Date Review Completed: ___/__/20___

General Comments: _____

_____

Student: _____ Grade: _____ Week Beginning: _____

Weekly Lesson Planner

Day	Bible	Quiz or Test	Main Concepts to Cover	Date Covered
Mon				
Tues				
Wed				
Thur				
Fri				

Specific concepts that still need to be reviewed/re-emphasized: _____
_____ Date Review Completed: __ / __ / 20 __

Day	Reading	Quiz or Test	Main Concepts to Cover	Date Covered
Mon				
Tues				
Wed				
Thur				
Fri				

Specific concepts that still need to be reviewed/re-emphasized: _____
_____ Date Review Completed: __ / __ / 20 __

Day	Spelling and Handwriting	Quiz or Test	Main Concepts to Cover	Date Covered
Mon				
Tues				
Wed				
Thur				
Fri				

Specific concepts that still need to be reviewed/re-emphasized: _____
_____ Date Review Completed: __ / __ / 20 __

Day	Grammar and Phonics	Quiz or Test	Main Concepts to Cover	Date Covered
Mon				
Tues				
Wed				
Thur				
Fri				

Specific concepts that still need to be reviewed/re-emphasized: _____
_____ Date Review Completed: __ / __ / 20 __

Day	History	Quiz or Test	Main Concepts to Cover	Date Covered
Mon				
Tues				
Wed				
Thur				
Fri				

Specific concepts that still need to be reviewed/re-emphasized: _____

_____ Date Review Completed: __/__/20__

Day	Science	Quiz or Test	Main Concepts to Cover	Date Covered
Mon				
Tues				
Wed				
Thur				
Fri				

Specific concepts that still need to be reviewed/re-emphasized: _____

_____ Date Review Completed: __/__/20__

Day	Math	Quiz or Test	Main Concepts to Cover	Date Covered
Mon				
Tues				
Wed				
Thur				
Fri				

Specific concepts that still need to be reviewed/re-emphasized: _____

_____ Date Review Completed: __/__/20__

Day	Other: _____	Quiz or Test	Main Concepts to Cover	Date Covered
Mon				
Tues				
Wed				
Thur				
Fri				

Specific concepts that still need to be reviewed/re-emphasized: _____

_____ Date Review Completed: __/__/20__

General Comments: _____

_____

Student: _____ Grade: _____ Week Beginning: _____

Weekly Lesson Planner

Day	Bible	Quiz or Test	Main Concepts to Cover	Date Covered
Mon				
Tues				
Wed				
Thur				
Fri				

Specific concepts that still need to be reviewed/re-emphasized: _____

_____ Date Review Completed: __ / __ / 20 __

Day	Reading	Quiz or Test	Main Concepts to Cover	Date Covered
Mon				
Tues				
Wed				
Thur				
Fri				

Specific concepts that still need to be reviewed/re-emphasized: _____

_____ Date Review Completed: __ / __ / 20 __

Day	Spelling and Handwriting	Quiz or Test	Main Concepts to Cover	Date Covered
Mon				
Tues				
Wed				
Thur				
Fri				

Specific concepts that still need to be reviewed/re-emphasized: _____

_____ Date Review Completed: __ / __ / 20 __

Day	Grammar and Phonics	Quiz or Test	Main Concepts to Cover	Date Covered
Mon				
Tues				
Wed				
Thur				
Fri				

Specific concepts that still need to be reviewed/re-emphasized: _____

_____ Date Review Completed: __ / __ / 20 __

Day	History	Quiz or Test	Main Concepts to Cover	Date Covered
Mon				
Tues				
Wed				
Thur				
Fri				

Specific concepts that still need to be reviewed/re-emphasized: _____

_____ Date Review Completed: __/__/20__

Day	Science	Quiz or Test	Main Concepts to Cover	Date Covered
Mon				
Tues				
Wed				
Thur				
Fri				

Specific concepts that still need to be reviewed/re-emphasized: _____

_____ Date Review Completed: __/__/20__

Day	Math	Quiz or Test	Main Concepts to Cover	Date Covered
Mon				
Tues				
Wed				
Thur				
Fri				

Specific concepts that still need to be reviewed/re-emphasized: _____

_____ Date Review Completed: __/__/20__

Day	Other: _____	Quiz or Test	Main Concepts to Cover	Date Covered
Mon				
Tues				
Wed				
Thur				
Fri				

Specific concepts that still need to be reviewed/re-emphasized: _____

_____ Date Review Completed: __/__/20__

General Comments: _____

_____

Student: _____ Grade: _____ Week Beginning: _____

Weekly Lesson Planner

Day	Bible	Quiz or Test	Main Concepts to Cover	Date Covered
Mon				
Tues				
Wed				
Thur				
Fri				

Specific concepts that still need to be reviewed/re-emphasized: _____
_____ Date Review Completed: _/_/20_

Day	Reading	Quiz or Test	Main Concepts to Cover	Date Covered
Mon				
Tues				
Wed				
Thur				
Fri				

Specific concepts that still need to be reviewed/re-emphasized: _____
_____ Date Review Completed: _/_/20_

Day	Spelling and Handwriting	Quiz or Test	Main Concepts to Cover	Date Covered
Mon				
Tues				
Wed				
Thur				
Fri				

Specific concepts that still need to be reviewed/re-emphasized: _____
_____ Date Review Completed: _/_/20_

Day	Grammar and Phonics	Quiz or Test	Main Concepts to Cover	Date Covered
Mon				
Tues				
Wed				
Thur				
Fri				

Specific concepts that still need to be reviewed/re-emphasized: _____
_____ Date Review Completed: _/_/20_

Day	History	Quiz or Test	Main Concepts to Cover	Date Covered
Mon				
Tues				
Wed				
Thur				
Fri				

Specific concepts that still need to be reviewed/re-emphasized: _____

_____ Date Review Completed: _/ _/ 20 _

Day	Science	Quiz or Test	Main Concepts to Cover	Date Covered
Mon				
Tues				
Wed				
Thur				
Fri				

Specific concepts that still need to be reviewed/re-emphasized: _____

_____ Date Review Completed: _/ _/ 20 _

Day	Math	Quiz or Test	Main Concepts to Cover	Date Covered
Mon				
Tues				
Wed				
Thur				
Fri				

Specific concepts that still need to be reviewed/re-emphasized: _____

_____ Date Review Completed: _/ _/ 20 _

Day	Other: _____	Quiz or Test	Main Concepts to Cover	Date Covered
Mon				
Tues				
Wed				
Thur				
Fri				

Specific concepts that still need to be reviewed/re-emphasized: _____

_____ Date Review Completed: _/ _/ 20 _

General Comments: _____

_____

Student: _____ Grade: _____ Week Beginning: _____

Weekly Lesson Planner

Day	Bible	Quiz or Test	Main Concepts to Cover	Date Covered
Mon				
Tues				
Wed				
Thur				
Fri				

Specific concepts that still need to be reviewed/re-emphasized: _____

_____ Date Review Completed: __/__/20__

Day	Reading	Quiz or Test	Main Concepts to Cover	Date Covered
Mon				
Tues				
Wed				
Thur				
Fri				

Specific concepts that still need to be reviewed/re-emphasized: _____

_____ Date Review Completed: __/__/20__

Day	Spelling and Handwriting	Quiz or Test	Main Concepts to Cover	Date Covered
Mon				
Tues				
Wed				
Thur				
Fri				

Specific concepts that still need to be reviewed/re-emphasized: _____

_____ Date Review Completed: __/__/20__

Day	Grammar and Phonics	Quiz or Test	Main Concepts to Cover	Date Covered
Mon				
Tues				
Wed				
Thur				
Fri				

Specific concepts that still need to be reviewed/re-emphasized: _____

_____ Date Review Completed: __/__/20__

Day	History	Quiz or Test	Main Concepts to Cover	Date Covered
Mon				
Tues				
Wed				
Thur				
Fri				

Specific concepts that still need to be reviewed/re-emphasized: _____

_____ Date Review Completed: __/__/20__

Day	Science	Quiz or Test	Main Concepts to Cover	Date Covered
Mon				
Tues				
Wed				
Thur				
Fri				

Specific concepts that still need to be reviewed/re-emphasized: _____

_____ Date Review Completed: __/__/20__

Day	Math	Quiz or Test	Main Concepts to Cover	Date Covered
Mon				
Tues				
Wed				
Thur				
Fri				

Specific concepts that still need to be reviewed/re-emphasized: _____

_____ Date Review Completed: __/__/20__

Day	Other: _____	Quiz or Test	Main Concepts to Cover	Date Covered
Mon				
Tues				
Wed				
Thur				
Fri				

Specific concepts that still need to be reviewed/re-emphasized: _____

_____ Date Review Completed: __/__/20__

General Comments: _____

_____

Student: _____ Grade: _____ Week Beginning: _____

Weekly Lesson Planner

Day	Bible	Quiz or Test	Main Concepts to Cover	Date Covered
Mon				
Tues				
Wed				
Thur				
Fri				

Specific concepts that still need to be reviewed/re-emphasized: _____

_____ Date Review Completed: __/__/20__

Day	Reading	Quiz or Test	Main Concepts to Cover	Date Covered
Mon				
Tues				
Wed				
Thur				
Fri				

Specific concepts that still need to be reviewed/re-emphasized: _____

_____ Date Review Completed: __/__/20__

Day	Spelling and Handwriting	Quiz or Test	Main Concepts to Cover	Date Covered
Mon				
Tues				
Wed				
Thur				
Fri				

Specific concepts that still need to be reviewed/re-emphasized: _____

_____ Date Review Completed: __/__/20__

Day	Grammar and Phonics	Quiz or Test	Main Concepts to Cover	Date Covered
Mon				
Tues				
Wed				
Thur				
Fri				

Specific concepts that still need to be reviewed/re-emphasized: _____

_____ Date Review Completed: __/__/20__

Day	History	Quiz or Test	Main Concepts to Cover	Date Covered
Mon				
Tues				
Wed				
Thur				
Fri				

Specific concepts that still need to be reviewed/re-emphasized: _____

_____ Date Review Completed: __/__/20__

Day	Science	Quiz or Test	Main Concepts to Cover	Date Covered
Mon				
Tues				
Wed				
Thur				
Fri				

Specific concepts that still need to be reviewed/re-emphasized: _____

_____ Date Review Completed: __/__/20__

Day	Math	Quiz or Test	Main Concepts to Cover	Date Covered
Mon				
Tues				
Wed				
Thur				
Fri				

Specific concepts that still need to be reviewed/re-emphasized: _____

_____ Date Review Completed: __/__/20__

Day	Other: _____	Quiz or Test	Main Concepts to Cover	Date Covered
Mon				
Tues				
Wed				
Thur				
Fri				

Specific concepts that still need to be reviewed/re-emphasized: _____

_____ Date Review Completed: __/__/20__

General Comments: _____

_____

Student: _____ Grade: _____ Week Beginning: _____

Weekly Lesson Planner

Day	Bible	Quiz or Test	Main Concepts to Cover	Date Covered
Mon				
Tues				
Wed				
Thur				
Fri				

Specific concepts that still need to be reviewed/re-emphasized: _____

_____ Date Review Completed: __/__/20__

Day	Reading	Quiz or Test	Main Concepts to Cover	Date Covered
Mon				
Tues				
Wed				
Thur				
Fri				

Specific concepts that still need to be reviewed/re-emphasized: _____

_____ Date Review Completed: __/__/20__

Day	Spelling and Handwriting	Quiz or Test	Main Concepts to Cover	Date Covered
Mon				
Tues				
Wed				
Thur				
Fri				

Specific concepts that still need to be reviewed/re-emphasized: _____

_____ Date Review Completed: __/__/20__

Day	Grammar and Phonics	Quiz or Test	Main Concepts to Cover	Date Covered
Mon				
Tues				
Wed				
Thur				
Fri				

Specific concepts that still need to be reviewed/re-emphasized: _____

_____ Date Review Completed: __/__/20__

Day	History	Quiz or Test	Main Concepts to Cover	Date Covered
Mon				
Tues				
Wed				
Thur				
Fri				

Specific concepts that still need to be reviewed/re-emphasized: _____

_____   Date Review Completed: _/_ / 20_

Day	Science	Quiz or Test	Main Concepts to Cover	Date Covered
Mon				
Tues				
Wed				
Thur				
Fri				

Specific concepts that still need to be reviewed/re-emphasized: _____

_____   Date Review Completed: _/_ / 20_

Day	Math	Quiz or Test	Main Concepts to Cover	Date Covered
Mon				
Tues				
Wed				
Thur				
Fri				

Specific concepts that still need to be reviewed/re-emphasized: _____

_____   Date Review Completed: _/_ / 20_

Day	Other: _____	Quiz or Test	Main Concepts to Cover	Date Covered
Mon				
Tues				
Wed				
Thur				
Fri				

Specific concepts that still need to be reviewed/re-emphasized: _____

_____   Date Review Completed: _/_ / 20_

General Comments: _____

_____

Student: _____ Grade: _____ Week Beginning: _____

Weekly Lesson Planner

Day	Bible	Quiz or Test	Main Concepts to Cover	Date Covered
Mon				
Tues				
Wed				
Thur				
Fri				

Specific concepts that still need to be reviewed/re-emphasized: _____

_____ Date Review Completed: __/__/20____

Day	Reading	Quiz or Test	Main Concepts to Cover	Date Covered
Mon				
Tues				
Wed				
Thur				
Fri				

Specific concepts that still need to be reviewed/re-emphasized: _____

_____ Date Review Completed: __/__/20____

Day	Spelling and Handwriting	Quiz or Test	Main Concepts to Cover	Date Covered
Mon				
Tues				
Wed				
Thur				
Fri				

Specific concepts that still need to be reviewed/re-emphasized: _____

_____ Date Review Completed: __/__/20____

Day	Grammar and Phonics	Quiz or Test	Main Concepts to Cover	Date Covered
Mon				
Tues				
Wed				
Thur				
Fri				

Specific concepts that still need to be reviewed/re-emphasized: _____

_____ Date Review Completed: __/__/20____

Day	History	Quiz or Test	Main Concepts to Cover	Date Covered
Mon				
Tues				
Wed				
Thur				
Fri				

Specific concepts that still need to be reviewed/re-emphasized: _____

_____ Date Review Completed: __/__/20__

Day	Science	Quiz or Test	Main Concepts to Cover	Date Covered
Mon				
Tues				
Wed				
Thur				
Fri				

Specific concepts that still need to be reviewed/re-emphasized: _____

_____ Date Review Completed: __/__/20__

Day	Math	Quiz or Test	Main Concepts to Cover	Date Covered
Mon				
Tues				
Wed				
Thur				
Fri				

Specific concepts that still need to be reviewed/re-emphasized: _____

_____ Date Review Completed: __/__/20__

Day	Other: _____	Quiz or Test	Main Concepts to Cover	Date Covered
Mon				
Tues				
Wed				
Thur				
Fri				

Specific concepts that still need to be reviewed/re-emphasized: _____

_____ Date Review Completed: __/__/20__

General Comments: _____

_____

Student: _____ Grade: _____ Week Beginning: _____

Weekly Lesson Planner

Day	Bible	Quiz or Test	Main Concepts to Cover	Date Covered
Mon				
Tues				
Wed				
Thur				
Fri				

Specific concepts that still need to be reviewed/re-emphasized: _____

_____ Date Review Completed: __/__/20__

Day	Reading	Quiz or Test	Main Concepts to Cover	Date Covered
Mon				
Tues				
Wed				
Thur				
Fri				

Specific concepts that still need to be reviewed/re-emphasized: _____

_____ Date Review Completed: __/__/20__

Day	Spelling and Handwriting	Quiz or Test	Main Concepts to Cover	Date Covered
Mon				
Tues				
Wed				
Thur				
Fri				

Specific concepts that still need to be reviewed/re-emphasized: _____

_____ Date Review Completed: __/__/20__

Day	Grammar and Phonics	Quiz or Test	Main Concepts to Cover	Date Covered
Mon				
Tues				
Wed				
Thur				
Fri				

Specific concepts that still need to be reviewed/re-emphasized: _____

_____ Date Review Completed: __/__/20__

Day	History	Quiz or Test	Main Concepts to Cover	Date Covered
Mon				
Tues				
Wed				
Thur				
Fri				

Specific concepts that still need to be reviewed/re-emphasized: _____
_____   Date Review Completed: __/__/20__

Day	Science	Quiz or Test	Main Concepts to Cover	Date Covered
Mon				
Tues				
Wed				
Thur				
Fri				

Specific concepts that still need to be reviewed/re-emphasized: _____
_____   Date Review Completed: __/__/20__

Day	Math	Quiz or Test	Main Concepts to Cover	Date Covered
Mon				
Tues				
Wed				
Thur				
Fri				

Specific concepts that still need to be reviewed/re-emphasized: _____
_____   Date Review Completed: __/__/20__

Day	Other: _____	Quiz or Test	Main Concepts to Cover	Date Covered
Mon				
Tues				
Wed				
Thur				
Fri				

Specific concepts that still need to be reviewed/re-emphasized: _____
_____   Date Review Completed: __/__/20__

General Comments: _____
_____

Student: _____ Grade: _____ Week Beginning: _____

Weekly Lesson Planner

Day	Bible	Quiz or Test	Main Concepts to Cover	Date Covered
Mon				
Tues				
Wed				
Thur				
Fri				

Specific concepts that still need to be reviewed/re-emphasized: _____
_____   Date Review Completed: __/__/20__

Day	Reading	Quiz or Test	Main Concepts to Cover	Date Covered
Mon				
Tues				
Wed				
Thur				
Fri				

Specific concepts that still need to be reviewed/re-emphasized: _____
_____   Date Review Completed: __/__/20__

Day	Spelling and Handwriting	Quiz or Test	Main Concepts to Cover	Date Covered
Mon				
Tues				
Wed				
Thur				
Fri				

Specific concepts that still need to be reviewed/re-emphasized: _____
_____   Date Review Completed: __/__/20__

Day	Grammar and Phonics	Quiz or Test	Main Concepts to Cover	Date Covered
Mon				
Tues				
Wed				
Thur				
Fri				

Specific concepts that still need to be reviewed/re-emphasized: _____
_____   Date Review Completed: __/__/20__

Day	History	Quiz or Test	Main Concepts to Cover	Date Covered
Mon				
Tues				
Wed				
Thur				
Fri				

Specific concepts that still need to be reviewed/re-emphasized: _____

_____ Date Review Completed: _/ / 20_

Day	Science	Quiz or Test	Main Concepts to Cover	Date Covered
Mon				
Tues				
Wed				
Thur				
Fri				

Specific concepts that still need to be reviewed/re-emphasized: _____

_____ Date Review Completed: _/ / 20_

Day	Math	Quiz or Test	Main Concepts to Cover	Date Covered
Mon				
Tues				
Wed				
Thur				
Fri				

Specific concepts that still need to be reviewed/re-emphasized: _____

_____ Date Review Completed: _/ / 20_

Day	Other: _____	Quiz or Test	Main Concepts to Cover	Date Covered
Mon				
Tues				
Wed				
Thur				
Fri				

Specific concepts that still need to be reviewed/re-emphasized: _____

_____ Date Review Completed: _/ / 20_

General Comments: _____

_____

Student: _____ Grade: _____ Week Beginning: _____

Weekly Lesson Planner

Day	Bible	Quiz or Test	Main Concepts to Cover	Date Covered
Mon				
Tues				
Wed				
Thur				
Fri				

Specific concepts that still need to be reviewed/re-emphasized: _____
_____ Date Review Completed: __/__/20__

Day	Reading	Quiz or Test	Main Concepts to Cover	Date Covered
Mon				
Tues				
Wed				
Thur				
Fri				

Specific concepts that still need to be reviewed/re-emphasized: _____
_____ Date Review Completed: __/__/20__

Day	Spelling and Handwriting	Quiz or Test	Main Concepts to Cover	Date Covered
Mon				
Tues				
Wed				
Thur				
Fri				

Specific concepts that still need to be reviewed/re-emphasized: _____
_____ Date Review Completed: __/__/20__

Day	Grammar and Phonics	Quiz or Test	Main Concepts to Cover	Date Covered
Mon				
Tues				
Wed				
Thur				
Fri				

Specific concepts that still need to be reviewed/re-emphasized: _____
_____ Date Review Completed: __/__/20__

Day	History	Quiz or Test	Main Concepts to Cover	Date Covered
Mon				
Tues				
Wed				
Thur				
Fri				

Specific concepts that still need to be reviewed/re-emphasized: _____

_____   Date Review Completed: __/__/20__

Day	Science	Quiz or Test	Main Concepts to Cover	Date Covered
Mon				
Tues				
Wed				
Thur				
Fri				

Specific concepts that still need to be reviewed/re-emphasized: _____

_____   Date Review Completed: __/__/20__

Day	Math	Quiz or Test	Main Concepts to Cover	Date Covered
Mon				
Tues				
Wed				
Thur				
Fri				

Specific concepts that still need to be reviewed/re-emphasized: _____

_____   Date Review Completed: __/__/20__

Day	Other: _____	Quiz or Test	Main Concepts to Cover	Date Covered
Mon				
Tues				
Wed				
Thur				
Fri				

Specific concepts that still need to be reviewed/re-emphasized: _____

_____   Date Review Completed: __/__/20__

General Comments: _____

_____

Student: _____ Grade: _____ Week Beginning: _____

Weekly Lesson Planner

Day	Bible	Quiz or Test	Main Concepts to Cover	Date Covered
Mon				
Tues				
Wed				
Thur				
Fri				

Specific concepts that still need to be reviewed/re-emphasized: _____

_____ Date Review Completed: __/__/20__

Day	Reading	Quiz or Test	Main Concepts to Cover	Date Covered
Mon				
Tues				
Wed				
Thur				
Fri				

Specific concepts that still need to be reviewed/re-emphasized: _____

_____ Date Review Completed: __/__/20__

Day	Spelling and Handwriting	Quiz or Test	Main Concepts to Cover	Date Covered
Mon				
Tues				
Wed				
Thur				
Fri				

Specific concepts that still need to be reviewed/re-emphasized: _____

_____ Date Review Completed: __/__/20__

Day	Grammar and Phonics	Quiz or Test	Main Concepts to Cover	Date Covered
Mon				
Tues				
Wed				
Thur				
Fri				

Specific concepts that still need to be reviewed/re-emphasized: _____

_____ Date Review Completed: __/__/20__

Day	History	Quiz or Test	Main Concepts to Cover	Date Covered
Mon				
Tues				
Wed				
Thur				
Fri				

Specific concepts that still need to be reviewed/re-emphasized: _____

_____ Date Review Completed: __/__/20__

Day	Science	Quiz or Test	Main Concepts to Cover	Date Covered
Mon				
Tues				
Wed				
Thur				
Fri				

Specific concepts that still need to be reviewed/re-emphasized: _____

_____ Date Review Completed: __/__/20__

Day	Math	Quiz or Test	Main Concepts to Cover	Date Covered
Mon				
Tues				
Wed				
Thur				
Fri				

Specific concepts that still need to be reviewed/re-emphasized: _____

_____ Date Review Completed: __/__/20__

Day	Other: _____	Quiz or Test	Main Concepts to Cover	Date Covered
Mon				
Tues				
Wed				
Thur				
Fri				

Specific concepts that still need to be reviewed/re-emphasized: _____

_____ Date Review Completed: __/__/20__

General Comments: _____

_____

Student: _____ Grade: _____ Week Beginning: _____

Weekly Lesson Planner

Day	Bible	Quiz or Test	Main Concepts to Cover	Date Covered
Mon				
Tues				
Wed				
Thur				
Fri				

Specific concepts that still need to be reviewed/re-emphasized: _____
_____ Date Review Completed: _/ / 20___

Day	Reading	Quiz or Test	Main Concepts to Cover	Date Covered
Mon				
Tues				
Wed				
Thur				
Fri				

Specific concepts that still need to be reviewed/re-emphasized: _____
_____ Date Review Completed: _/ / 20___

Day	Spelling and Handwriting	Quiz or Test	Main Concepts to Cover	Date Covered
Mon				
Tues				
Wed				
Thur				
Fri				

Specific concepts that still need to be reviewed/re-emphasized: _____
_____ Date Review Completed: _/ / 20___

Day	Grammar and Phonics	Quiz or Test	Main Concepts to Cover	Date Covered
Mon				
Tues				
Wed				
Thur				
Fri				

Specific concepts that still need to be reviewed/re-emphasized: _____
_____ Date Review Completed: _/ / 20___

Day	History	Quiz or Test	Main Concepts to Cover	Date Covered
Mon				
Tues				
Wed				
Thur				
Fri				

Specific concepts that still need to be reviewed/re-emphasized: _____
_____   Date Review Completed: _/_ / 20 __

Day	Science	Quiz or Test	Main Concepts to Cover	Date Covered
Mon				
Tues				
Wed				
Thur				
Fri				

Specific concepts that still need to be reviewed/re-emphasized: _____
_____   Date Review Completed: _/_ / 20 __

Day	Math	Quiz or Test	Main Concepts to Cover	Date Covered
Mon				
Tues				
Wed				
Thur				
Fri				

Specific concepts that still need to be reviewed/re-emphasized: _____
_____   Date Review Completed: _/_ / 20 __

Day	Other: _____	Quiz or Test	Main Concepts to Cover	Date Covered
Mon				
Tues				
Wed				
Thur				
Fri				

Specific concepts that still need to be reviewed/re-emphasized: _____
_____   Date Review Completed: _/_ / 20 __

General Comments: _____
_____

Student: _____ Grade: _____ Week Beginning: _____

Weekly Lesson Planner

Day	Bible	Quiz or Test	Main Concepts to Cover	Date Covered
Mon				
Tues				
Wed				
Thur				
Fri				

Specific concepts that still need to be reviewed/re-emphasized: _____

_____ Date Review Completed: ___ / ___ / 20 ___

Day	Reading	Quiz or Test	Main Concepts to Cover	Date Covered
Mon				
Tues				
Wed				
Thur				
Fri				

Specific concepts that still need to be reviewed/re-emphasized: _____

_____ Date Review Completed: ___ / ___ / 20 ___

Day	Spelling and Handwriting	Quiz or Test	Main Concepts to Cover	Date Covered
Mon				
Tues				
Wed				
Thur				
Fri				

Specific concepts that still need to be reviewed/re-emphasized: _____

_____ Date Review Completed: ___ / ___ / 20 ___

Day	Grammar and Phonics	Quiz or Test	Main Concepts to Cover	Date Covered
Mon				
Tues				
Wed				
Thur				
Fri				

Specific concepts that still need to be reviewed/re-emphasized: _____

_____ Date Review Completed: ___ / ___ / 20 ___

Day	History	Quiz or Test	Main Concepts to Cover	Date Covered
Mon				
Tues				
Wed				
Thur				
Fri				

Specific concepts that still need to be reviewed/re-emphasized: _____
_____   Date Review Completed: __ / __ / 20 __

Day	Science	Quiz or Test	Main Concepts to Cover	Date Covered
Mon				
Tues				
Wed				
Thur				
Fri				

Specific concepts that still need to be reviewed/re-emphasized: _____
_____   Date Review Completed: __ / __ / 20 __

Day	Math	Quiz or Test	Main Concepts to Cover	Date Covered
Mon				
Tues				
Wed				
Thur				
Fri				

Specific concepts that still need to be reviewed/re-emphasized: _____
_____   Date Review Completed: __ / __ / 20 __

Day	Other: _____	Quiz or Test	Main Concepts to Cover	Date Covered
Mon				
Tues				
Wed				
Thur				
Fri				

Specific concepts that still need to be reviewed/re-emphasized: _____
_____   Date Review Completed: __ / __ / 20 __

General Comments: _____
_____

Student: _____ Grade: _____ Week Beginning: _____

Weekly Lesson Planner

Day	Bible	Quiz or Test	Main Concepts to Cover	Date Covered
Mon				
Tues				
Wed				
Thur				
Fri				

Specific concepts that still need to be reviewed/re-emphasized: _____

_____ Date Review Completed: __/__/20__

Day	Reading	Quiz or Test	Main Concepts to Cover	Date Covered
Mon				
Tues				
Wed				
Thur				
Fri				

Specific concepts that still need to be reviewed/re-emphasized: _____

_____ Date Review Completed: __/__/20__

Day	Spelling and Handwriting	Quiz or Test	Main Concepts to Cover	Date Covered
Mon				
Tues				
Wed				
Thur				
Fri				

Specific concepts that still need to be reviewed/re-emphasized: _____

_____ Date Review Completed: __/__/20__

Day	Grammar and Phonics	Quiz or Test	Main Concepts to Cover	Date Covered
Mon				
Tues				
Wed				
Thur				
Fri				

Specific concepts that still need to be reviewed/re-emphasized: _____

_____ Date Review Completed: __/__/20__

Day	History	Quiz or Test	Main Concepts to Cover	Date Covered
Mon				
Tues				
Wed				
Thur				
Fri				

Specific concepts that still need to be reviewed/re-emphasized: _____

_____   Date Review Completed: __/__/20__

Day	Science	Quiz or Test	Main Concepts to Cover	Date Covered
Mon				
Tues				
Wed				
Thur				
Fri				

Specific concepts that still need to be reviewed/re-emphasized: _____

_____   Date Review Completed: __/__/20__

Day	Math	Quiz or Test	Main Concepts to Cover	Date Covered
Mon				
Tues				
Wed				
Thur				
Fri				

Specific concepts that still need to be reviewed/re-emphasized: _____

_____   Date Review Completed: __/__/20__

Day	Other: _____	Quiz or Test	Main Concepts to Cover	Date Covered
Mon				
Tues				
Wed				
Thur				
Fri				

Specific concepts that still need to be reviewed/re-emphasized: _____

_____   Date Review Completed: __/__/20__

General Comments: _____

_____

Student: _____ Grade: _____ Week Beginning: _____

Weekly Lesson Planner

Day	Bible	Quiz or Test	Main Concepts to Cover	Date Covered
Mon				
Tues				
Wed				
Thur				
Fri				

Specific concepts that still need to be reviewed/re-emphasized: _____

_____ Date Review Completed: ___/___/20___

Day	Reading	Quiz or Test	Main Concepts to Cover	Date Covered
Mon				
Tues				
Wed				
Thur				
Fri				

Specific concepts that still need to be reviewed/re-emphasized: _____

_____ Date Review Completed: ___/___/20___

Day	Spelling and Handwriting	Quiz or Test	Main Concepts to Cover	Date Covered
Mon				
Tues				
Wed				
Thur				
Fri				

Specific concepts that still need to be reviewed/re-emphasized: _____

_____ Date Review Completed: ___/___/20___

Day	Grammar and Phonics	Quiz or Test	Main Concepts to Cover	Date Covered
Mon				
Tues				
Wed				
Thur				
Fri				

Specific concepts that still need to be reviewed/re-emphasized: _____

_____ Date Review Completed: ___/___/20___

Day	History	Quiz or Test	Main Concepts to Cover	Date Covered
Mon				
Tues				
Wed				
Thur				
Fri				

Specific concepts that still need to be reviewed/re-emphasized: _____
_____ Date Review Completed: _/_/20_

Day	Science	Quiz or Test	Main Concepts to Cover	Date Covered
Mon				
Tues				
Wed				
Thur				
Fri				

Specific concepts that still need to be reviewed/re-emphasized: _____
_____ Date Review Completed: _/_/20_

Day	Math	Quiz or Test	Main Concepts to Cover	Date Covered
Mon				
Tues				
Wed				
Thur				
Fri				

Specific concepts that still need to be reviewed/re-emphasized: _____
_____ Date Review Completed: _/_/20_

Day	Other: _____	Quiz or Test	Main Concepts to Cover	Date Covered
Mon				
Tues				
Wed				
Thur				
Fri				

Specific concepts that still need to be reviewed/re-emphasized: _____
_____ Date Review Completed: _/_/20_

General Comments: _____
_____

Student: _____ Grade: _____ Week Beginning: _____

Weekly Lesson Planner

Day	Bible	Quiz or Test	Main Concepts to Cover	Date Covered
Mon				
Tues				
Wed				
Thur				
Fri				

Specific concepts that still need to be reviewed/re-emphasized: _____

_____ Date Review Completed: __/__/20__

Day	Reading	Quiz or Test	Main Concepts to Cover	Date Covered
Mon				
Tues				
Wed				
Thur				
Fri				

Specific concepts that still need to be reviewed/re-emphasized: _____

_____ Date Review Completed: __/__/20__

Day	Spelling and Handwriting	Quiz or Test	Main Concepts to Cover	Date Covered
Mon				
Tues				
Wed				
Thur				
Fri				

Specific concepts that still need to be reviewed/re-emphasized: _____

_____ Date Review Completed: __/__/20__

Day	Grammar and Phonics	Quiz or Test	Main Concepts to Cover	Date Covered
Mon				
Tues				
Wed				
Thur				
Fri				

Specific concepts that still need to be reviewed/re-emphasized: _____

_____ Date Review Completed: __/__/20__

Day	History	Quiz or Test	Main Concepts to Cover	Date Covered
Mon				
Tues				
Wed				
Thur				
Fri				

Specific concepts that still need to be reviewed/re-emphasized: _____

_____ Date Review Completed: __/__/20__

Day	Science	Quiz or Test	Main Concepts to Cover	Date Covered
Mon				
Tues				
Wed				
Thur				
Fri				

Specific concepts that still need to be reviewed/re-emphasized: _____

_____ Date Review Completed: __/__/20__

Day	Math	Quiz or Test	Main Concepts to Cover	Date Covered
Mon				
Tues				
Wed				
Thur				
Fri				

Specific concepts that still need to be reviewed/re-emphasized: _____

_____ Date Review Completed: __/__/20__

Day	Other: _____	Quiz or Test	Main Concepts to Cover	Date Covered
Mon				
Tues				
Wed				
Thur				
Fri				

Specific concepts that still need to be reviewed/re-emphasized: _____

_____ Date Review Completed: __/__/20__

General Comments: _____

_____

Student: _____ Grade: _____ Week Beginning: _____

Weekly Lesson Planner

Day	Bible	Quiz or Test	Main Concepts to Cover	Date Covered
Mon				
Tues				
Wed				
Thur				
Fri				

Specific concepts that still need to be reviewed/re-emphasized: _____
_____   Date Review Completed: _/_/20__

Day	Reading	Quiz or Test	Main Concepts to Cover	Date Covered
Mon				
Tues				
Wed				
Thur				
Fri				

Specific concepts that still need to be reviewed/re-emphasized: _____
_____   Date Review Completed: _/_/20__

Day	Spelling and Handwriting	Quiz or Test	Main Concepts to Cover	Date Covered
Mon				
Tues				
Wed				
Thur				
Fri				

Specific concepts that still need to be reviewed/re-emphasized: _____
_____   Date Review Completed: _/_/20__

Day	Grammar and Phonics	Quiz or Test	Main Concepts to Cover	Date Covered
Mon				
Tues				
Wed				
Thur				
Fri				

Specific concepts that still need to be reviewed/re-emphasized: _____
_____   Date Review Completed: _/_/20__

Day	History	Quiz or Test	Main Concepts to Cover	Date Covered
Mon				
Tues				
Wed				
Thur				
Fri				

Specific concepts that still need to be reviewed/re-emphasized: _____

_____   Date Review Completed: __/__/20__

Day	Science	Quiz or Test	Main Concepts to Cover	Date Covered
Mon				
Tues				
Wed				
Thur				
Fri				

Specific concepts that still need to be reviewed/re-emphasized: _____

_____   Date Review Completed: __/__/20__

Day	Math	Quiz or Test	Main Concepts to Cover	Date Covered
Mon				
Tues				
Wed				
Thur				
Fri				

Specific concepts that still need to be reviewed/re-emphasized: _____

_____   Date Review Completed: __/__/20__

Day	Other: _____	Quiz or Test	Main Concepts to Cover	Date Covered
Mon				
Tues				
Wed				
Thur				
Fri				

Specific concepts that still need to be reviewed/re-emphasized: _____

_____   Date Review Completed: __/__/20__

General Comments: _____

_____

Student: _____ Grade: _____ Week Beginning: _____

Weekly Lesson Planner

Day	Bible	Quiz or Test	Main Concepts to Cover	Date Covered
Mon				
Tues				
Wed				
Thur				
Fri				

Specific concepts that still need to be reviewed/re-emphasized: _____
_____ Date Review Completed: __/__/20__

Day	Reading	Quiz or Test	Main Concepts to Cover	Date Covered
Mon				
Tues				
Wed				
Thur				
Fri				

Specific concepts that still need to be reviewed/re-emphasized: _____
_____ Date Review Completed: __/__/20__

Day	Spelling and Handwriting	Quiz or Test	Main Concepts to Cover	Date Covered
Mon				
Tues				
Wed				
Thur				
Fri				

Specific concepts that still need to be reviewed/re-emphasized: _____
_____ Date Review Completed: __/__/20__

Day	Grammar and Phonics	Quiz or Test	Main Concepts to Cover	Date Covered
Mon				
Tues				
Wed				
Thur				
Fri				

Specific concepts that still need to be reviewed/re-emphasized: _____
_____ Date Review Completed: __/__/20__

Day	History	Quiz or Test	Main Concepts to Cover	Date Covered
Mon				
Tues				
Wed				
Thur				
Fri				

Specific concepts that still need to be reviewed/re-emphasized: _____

_____   Date Review Completed: __/__/20____

Day	Science	Quiz or Test	Main Concepts to Cover	Date Covered
Mon				
Tues				
Wed				
Thur				
Fri				

Specific concepts that still need to be reviewed/re-emphasized: _____

_____   Date Review Completed: __/__/20____

Day	Math	Quiz or Test	Main Concepts to Cover	Date Covered
Mon				
Tues				
Wed				
Thur				
Fri				

Specific concepts that still need to be reviewed/re-emphasized: _____

_____   Date Review Completed: __/__/20____

Day	Other: _____	Quiz or Test	Main Concepts to Cover	Date Covered
Mon				
Tues				
Wed				
Thur				
Fri				

Specific concepts that still need to be reviewed/re-emphasized: _____

_____   Date Review Completed: __/__/20____

General Comments: _____

_____

Student: _____ Grade: _____ Week Beginning: _____

Weekly Lesson Planner

Day	Bible	Quiz or Test	Main Concepts to Cover	Date Covered
Mon				
Tues				
Wed				
Thur				
Fri				

Specific concepts that still need to be reviewed/re-emphasized: _____

_____ Date Review Completed: ___/ / 20 ___

Day	Reading	Quiz or Test	Main Concepts to Cover	Date Covered
Mon				
Tues				
Wed				
Thur				
Fri				

Specific concepts that still need to be reviewed/re-emphasized: _____

_____ Date Review Completed: ___/ / 20 ___

Day	Spelling and Handwriting	Quiz or Test	Main Concepts to Cover	Date Covered
Mon				
Tues				
Wed				
Thur				
Fri				

Specific concepts that still need to be reviewed/re-emphasized: _____

_____ Date Review Completed: ___/ / 20 ___

Day	Grammar and Phonics	Quiz or Test	Main Concepts to Cover	Date Covered
Mon				
Tues				
Wed				
Thur				
Fri				

Specific concepts that still need to be reviewed/re-emphasized: _____

_____ Date Review Completed: ___/ / 20 ___

Day	History	Quiz or Test	Main Concepts to Cover	Date Covered
Mon				
Tues				
Wed				
Thur				
Fri				

Specific concepts that still need to be reviewed/re-emphasized: _____

_____ Date Review Completed: __/__/20__

Day	Science	Quiz or Test	Main Concepts to Cover	Date Covered
Mon				
Tues				
Wed				
Thur				
Fri				

Specific concepts that still need to be reviewed/re-emphasized: _____

_____ Date Review Completed: __/__/20__

Day	Math	Quiz or Test	Main Concepts to Cover	Date Covered
Mon				
Tues				
Wed				
Thur				
Fri				

Specific concepts that still need to be reviewed/re-emphasized: _____

_____ Date Review Completed: __/__/20__

Day	Other: _____	Quiz or Test	Main Concepts to Cover	Date Covered
Mon				
Tues				
Wed				
Thur				
Fri				

Specific concepts that still need to be reviewed/re-emphasized: _____

_____ Date Review Completed: __/__/20__

General Comments: _____

_____

Student: _____ Grade: _____ Week Beginning: _____

Weekly Lesson Planner

Day	Bible	Quiz or Test	Main Concepts to Cover	Date Covered
Mon				
Tues				
Wed				
Thur				
Fri				

Specific concepts that still need to be reviewed/re-emphasized: _____

_____ Date Review Completed: __/__/20__

Day	Reading	Quiz or Test	Main Concepts to Cover	Date Covered
Mon				
Tues				
Wed				
Thur				
Fri				

Specific concepts that still need to be reviewed/re-emphasized: _____

_____ Date Review Completed: __/__/20__

Day	Spelling and Handwriting	Quiz or Test	Main Concepts to Cover	Date Covered
Mon				
Tues				
Wed				
Thur				
Fri				

Specific concepts that still need to be reviewed/re-emphasized: _____

_____ Date Review Completed: __/__/20__

Day	Grammar and Phonics	Quiz or Test	Main Concepts to Cover	Date Covered
Mon				
Tues				
Wed				
Thur				
Fri				

Specific concepts that still need to be reviewed/re-emphasized: _____

_____ Date Review Completed: __/__/20__

Day	History	Quiz or Test	Main Concepts to Cover	Date Covered
Mon				
Tues				
Wed				
Thur				
Fri				

Specific concepts that still need to be reviewed/re-emphasized: _____

_____ Date Review Completed: ___ / ___ / 20 ___

Day	Science	Quiz or Test	Main Concepts to Cover	Date Covered
Mon				
Tues				
Wed				
Thur				
Fri				

Specific concepts that still need to be reviewed/re-emphasized: _____

_____ Date Review Completed: ___ / ___ / 20 ___

Day	Math	Quiz or Test	Main Concepts to Cover	Date Covered
Mon				
Tues				
Wed				
Thur				
Fri				

Specific concepts that still need to be reviewed/re-emphasized: _____

_____ Date Review Completed: ___ / ___ / 20 ___

Day	Other: _____	Quiz or Test	Main Concepts to Cover	Date Covered
Mon				
Tues				
Wed				
Thur				
Fri				

Specific concepts that still need to be reviewed/re-emphasized: _____

_____ Date Review Completed: ___ / ___ / 20 ___

General Comments: _____

_____

Student: _____   Grade: _____   Week Beginning: _____

Weekly Lesson Planner

Day	Bible	Quiz or Test	Main Concepts to Cover	Date Covered
Mon				
Tues				
Wed				
Thur				
Fri				

Specific concepts that still need to be reviewed/re-emphasized: _____
_____   Date Review Completed: _/_/20__

Day	Reading	Quiz or Test	Main Concepts to Cover	Date Covered
Mon				
Tues				
Wed				
Thur				
Fri				

Specific concepts that still need to be reviewed/re-emphasized: _____
_____   Date Review Completed: _/_/20__

Day	Spelling and Handwriting	Quiz or Test	Main Concepts to Cover	Date Covered
Mon				
Tues				
Wed				
Thur				
Fri				

Specific concepts that still need to be reviewed/re-emphasized: _____
_____   Date Review Completed: _/_/20__

Day	Grammar and Phonics	Quiz or Test	Main Concepts to Cover	Date Covered
Mon				
Tues				
Wed				
Thur				
Fri				

Specific concepts that still need to be reviewed/re-emphasized: _____
_____   Date Review Completed: _/_/20__

Day	History	Quiz or Test	Main Concepts to Cover	Date Covered
Mon				
Tues				
Wed				
Thur				
Fri				

Specific concepts that still need to be reviewed/re-emphasized: _____

_____ Date Review Completed: __/__/20__

Day	Science	Quiz or Test	Main Concepts to Cover	Date Covered
Mon				
Tues				
Wed				
Thur				
Fri				

Specific concepts that still need to be reviewed/re-emphasized: _____

_____ Date Review Completed: __/__/20__

Day	Math	Quiz or Test	Main Concepts to Cover	Date Covered
Mon				
Tues				
Wed				
Thur				
Fri				

Specific concepts that still need to be reviewed/re-emphasized: _____

_____ Date Review Completed: __/__/20__

Day	Other: _____	Quiz or Test	Main Concepts to Cover	Date Covered
Mon				
Tues				
Wed				
Thur				
Fri				

Specific concepts that still need to be reviewed/re-emphasized: _____

_____ Date Review Completed: __/__/20__

General Comments: _____

_____

Student: _____ Grade: _____ Week Beginning: _____

Weekly Lesson Planner

Day	Bible	Quiz or Test	Main Concepts to Cover	Date Covered
Mon				
Tues				
Wed				
Thur				
Fri				

Specific concepts that still need to be reviewed/re-emphasized: _____

_____ Date Review Completed: _/_/20__

Day	Reading	Quiz or Test	Main Concepts to Cover	Date Covered
Mon				
Tues				
Wed				
Thur				
Fri				

Specific concepts that still need to be reviewed/re-emphasized: _____

_____ Date Review Completed: _/_/20__

Day	Spelling and Handwriting	Quiz or Test	Main Concepts to Cover	Date Covered
Mon				
Tues				
Wed				
Thur				
Fri				

Specific concepts that still need to be reviewed/re-emphasized: _____

_____ Date Review Completed: _/_/20__

Day	Grammar and Phonics	Quiz or Test	Main Concepts to Cover	Date Covered
Mon				
Tues				
Wed				
Thur				
Fri				

Specific concepts that still need to be reviewed/re-emphasized: _____

_____ Date Review Completed: _/_/20__

Day	History	Quiz or Test	Main Concepts to Cover	Date Covered
Mon				
Tues				
Wed				
Thur				
Fri				

Specific concepts that still need to be reviewed/re-emphasized: _____

_____ Date Review Completed: __/__/20__

Day	Science	Quiz or Test	Main Concepts to Cover	Date Covered
Mon				
Tues				
Wed				
Thur				
Fri				

Specific concepts that still need to be reviewed/re-emphasized: _____

_____ Date Review Completed: __/__/20__

Day	Math	Quiz or Test	Main Concepts to Cover	Date Covered
Mon				
Tues				
Wed				
Thur				
Fri				

Specific concepts that still need to be reviewed/re-emphasized: _____

_____ Date Review Completed: __/__/20__

Day	Other: _____	Quiz or Test	Main Concepts to Cover	Date Covered
Mon				
Tues				
Wed				
Thur				
Fri				

Specific concepts that still need to be reviewed/re-emphasized: _____

_____ Date Review Completed: __/__/20__

General Comments: _____

_____

Student: _____ Grade: _____ Week Beginning: _____

Weekly Lesson Planner

Day	Bible	Quiz or Test	Main Concepts to Cover	Date Covered
Mon				
Tues				
Wed				
Thur				
Fri				

Specific concepts that still need to be reviewed/re-emphasized: _____
_____ Date Review Completed: ___ / ___ / 20 ___

Day	Reading	Quiz or Test	Main Concepts to Cover	Date Covered
Mon				
Tues				
Wed				
Thur				
Fri				

Specific concepts that still need to be reviewed/re-emphasized: _____
_____ Date Review Completed: ___ / ___ / 20 ___

Day	Spelling and Handwriting	Quiz or Test	Main Concepts to Cover	Date Covered
Mon				
Tues				
Wed				
Thur				
Fri				

Specific concepts that still need to be reviewed/re-emphasized: _____
_____ Date Review Completed: ___ / ___ / 20 ___

Day	Grammar and Phonics	Quiz or Test	Main Concepts to Cover	Date Covered
Mon				
Tues				
Wed				
Thur				
Fri				

Specific concepts that still need to be reviewed/re-emphasized: _____
Date Review Completed: ___ / ___ / 20 ___

Day	History	Quiz or Test	Main Concepts to Cover	Date Covered
Mon				
Tues				
Wed				
Thur				
Fri				

Specific concepts that still need to be reviewed/re-emphasized: _____
_____   Date Review Completed: _/_/20__

Day	Science	Quiz or Test	Main Concepts to Cover	Date Covered
Mon				
Tues				
Wed				
Thur				
Fri				

Specific concepts that still need to be reviewed/re-emphasized: _____
_____   Date Review Completed: _/_/20__

Day	Math	Quiz or Test	Main Concepts to Cover	Date Covered
Mon				
Tues				
Wed				
Thur				
Fri				

Specific concepts that still need to be reviewed/re-emphasized: _____
_____   Date Review Completed: _/_/20__

Day	Other: _____	Quiz or Test	Main Concepts to Cover	Date Covered
Mon				
Tues				
Wed				
Thur				
Fri				

Specific concepts that still need to be reviewed/re-emphasized: _____
_____   Date Review Completed: _/_/20__

General Comments: _____
_____

Student: _____ Grade: _____ Week Beginning: _____

Weekly Lesson Planner

Day	Bible	Quiz or Test	Main Concepts to Cover	Date Covered
Mon				
Tues				
Wed				
Thur				
Fri				

Specific concepts that still need to be reviewed/re-emphasized: _____
_____   Date Review Completed: _/_/20_

Day	Reading	Quiz or Test	Main Concepts to Cover	Date Covered
Mon				
Tues				
Wed				
Thur				
Fri				

Specific concepts that still need to be reviewed/re-emphasized: _____
_____   Date Review Completed: _/_/20_

Day	Spelling and Handwriting	Quiz or Test	Main Concepts to Cover	Date Covered
Mon				
Tues				
Wed				
Thur				
Fri				

Specific concepts that still need to be reviewed/re-emphasized: _____
_____   Date Review Completed: _/_/20_

Day	Grammar and Phonics	Quiz or Test	Main Concepts to Cover	Date Covered
Mon				
Tues				
Wed				
Thur				
Fri				

Specific concepts that still need to be reviewed/re-emphasized: _____
_____   Date Review Completed: _/_/20_

Day	History	Quiz or Test	Main Concepts to Cover	Date Covered
Mon				
Tues				
Wed				
Thur				
Fri				

Specific concepts that still need to be reviewed/re-emphasized: _____

_____ Date Review Completed: __/__/20__

Day	Science	Quiz or Test	Main Concepts to Cover	Date Covered
Mon				
Tues				
Wed				
Thur				
Fri				

Specific concepts that still need to be reviewed/re-emphasized: _____

_____ Date Review Completed: __/__/20__

Day	Math	Quiz or Test	Main Concepts to Cover	Date Covered
Mon				
Tues				
Wed				
Thur				
Fri				

Specific concepts that still need to be reviewed/re-emphasized: _____

_____ Date Review Completed: __/__/20__

Day	Other: _____	Quiz or Test	Main Concepts to Cover	Date Covered
Mon				
Tues				
Wed				
Thur				
Fri				

Specific concepts that still need to be reviewed/re-emphasized: _____

_____ Date Review Completed: __/__/20__

General Comments: _____

_____

Student: _____ Grade: _____ Week Beginning: _____

Weekly Lesson Planner

Day	Bible	Quiz or Test	Main Concepts to Cover	Date Covered
Mon				
Tues				
Wed				
Thur				
Fri				

Specific concepts that still need to be reviewed/re-emphasized: _____
_____   Date Review Completed: __/__/20__

Day	Reading	Quiz or Test	Main Concepts to Cover	Date Covered
Mon				
Tues				
Wed				
Thur				
Fri				

Specific concepts that still need to be reviewed/re-emphasized: _____
_____   Date Review Completed: __/__/20__

Day	Spelling and Handwriting	Quiz or Test	Main Concepts to Cover	Date Covered
Mon				
Tues				
Wed				
Thur				
Fri				

Specific concepts that still need to be reviewed/re-emphasized: _____
_____   Date Review Completed: __/__/20__

Day	Grammar and Phonics	Quiz or Test	Main Concepts to Cover	Date Covered
Mon				
Tues				
Wed				
Thur				
Fri				

Specific concepts that still need to be reviewed/re-emphasized: _____
_____   Date Review Completed: __/__/20__

Day	History	Quiz or Test	Main Concepts to Cover	Date Covered
Mon				
Tues				
Wed				
Thur				
Fri				

Specific concepts that still need to be reviewed/re-emphasized: _____

_____   Date Review Completed: __ / __ / 20 __

Day	Science	Quiz or Test	Main Concepts to Cover	Date Covered
Mon				
Tues				
Wed				
Thur				
Fri				

Specific concepts that still need to be reviewed/re-emphasized: _____

_____   Date Review Completed: __ / __ / 20 __

Day	Math	Quiz or Test	Main Concepts to Cover	Date Covered
Mon				
Tues				
Wed				
Thur				
Fri				

Specific concepts that still need to be reviewed/re-emphasized: _____

_____   Date Review Completed: __ / __ / 20 __

Day	Other: _____	Quiz or Test	Main Concepts to Cover	Date Covered
Mon				
Tues				
Wed				
Thur				
Fri				

Specific concepts that still need to be reviewed/re-emphasized: _____

_____   Date Review Completed: __ / __ / 20 __

General Comments: _____

_____

Student: _____   Grade: _____   Week Beginning: _____

Weekly Lesson Planner

Day	Bible	Quiz or Test	Main Concepts to Cover	Date Covered
Mon				
Tues				
Wed				
Thur				
Fri				

Specific concepts that still need to be reviewed/re-emphasized: _____

_____   Date Review Completed: _/ / 20_

Day	Reading	Quiz or Test	Main Concepts to Cover	Date Covered
Mon				
Tues				
Wed				
Thur				
Fri				

Specific concepts that still need to be reviewed/re-emphasized: _____

_____   Date Review Completed: _/ / 20_

Day	Spelling and Handwriting	Quiz or Test	Main Concepts to Cover	Date Covered
Mon				
Tues				
Wed				
Thur				
Fri				

Specific concepts that still need to be reviewed/re-emphasized: _____

_____   Date Review Completed: _/ / 20_

Day	Grammar and Phonics	Quiz or Test	Main Concepts to Cover	Date Covered
Mon				
Tues				
Wed				
Thur				
Fri				

Specific concepts that still need to be reviewed/re-emphasized: _____

_____   Date Review Completed: _/ / 20_

Day	History	Quiz or Test	Main Concepts to Cover	Date Covered
Mon				
Tues				
Wed				
Thur				
Fri				

Specific concepts that still need to be reviewed/re-emphasized: _____

_____   Date Review Completed: _/ / 20_

Day	Science	Quiz or Test	Main Concepts to Cover	Date Covered
Mon				
Tues				
Wed				
Thur				
Fri				

Specific concepts that still need to be reviewed/re-emphasized: _____

_____   Date Review Completed: _/ / 20_

Day	Math	Quiz or Test	Main Concepts to Cover	Date Covered
Mon				
Tues				
Wed				
Thur				
Fri				

Specific concepts that still need to be reviewed/re-emphasized: _____

_____   Date Review Completed: _/ / 20_

Day	Other: _____	Quiz or Test	Main Concepts to Cover	Date Covered
Mon				
Tues				
Wed				
Thur				
Fri				

Specific concepts that still need to be reviewed/re-emphasized: _____

_____   Date Review Completed: _/ / 20_

General Comments: _____

_____

Student: _____ Grade: _____ Week Beginning: _____

Weekly Lesson Planner

Day	Bible	Quiz or Test	Main Concepts to Cover	Date Covered
Mon				
Tues				
Wed				
Thur				
Fri				

Specific concepts that still need to be reviewed/re-emphasized: _____

_____ Date Review Completed: __/__/20__

Day	Reading	Quiz or Test	Main Concepts to Cover	Date Covered
Mon				
Tues				
Wed				
Thur				
Fri				

Specific concepts that still need to be reviewed/re-emphasized: _____

_____ Date Review Completed: __/__/20__

Day	Spelling and Handwriting	Quiz or Test	Main Concepts to Cover	Date Covered
Mon				
Tues				
Wed				
Thur				
Fri				

Specific concepts that still need to be reviewed/re-emphasized: _____

_____ Date Review Completed: __/__/20__

Day	Grammar and Phonics	Quiz or Test	Main Concepts to Cover	Date Covered
Mon				
Tues				
Wed				
Thur				
Fri				

Specific concepts that still need to be reviewed/re-emphasized: _____

_____ Date Review Completed: __/__/20__

Day	History	Quiz or Test	Main Concepts to Cover	Date Covered
Mon				
Tues				
Wed				
Thur				
Fri				

Specific concepts that still need to be reviewed/re-emphasized: _____
_____ Date Review Completed: __/__/20__

Day	Science	Quiz or Test	Main Concepts to Cover	Date Covered
Mon				
Tues				
Wed				
Thur				
Fri				

Specific concepts that still need to be reviewed/re-emphasized: _____
_____ Date Review Completed: __/__/20__

Day	Math	Quiz or Test	Main Concepts to Cover	Date Covered
Mon				
Tues				
Wed				
Thur				
Fri				

Specific concepts that still need to be reviewed/re-emphasized: _____
_____ Date Review Completed: __/__/20__

Day	Other: _____	Quiz or Test	Main Concepts to Cover	Date Covered
Mon				
Tues				
Wed				
Thur				
Fri				

Specific concepts that still need to be reviewed/re-emphasized: _____
_____ Date Review Completed: __/__/20__

General Comments: _____
_____

Student: _____ Grade: _____ Week Beginning: _____

Weekly Lesson Planner

Day	Bible	Quiz or Test	Main Concepts to Cover	Date Covered
Mon				
Tues				
Wed				
Thur				
Fri				

Specific concepts that still need to be reviewed/re-emphasized: _____
_____ Date Review Completed: __/__/20__

Day	Reading	Quiz or Test	Main Concepts to Cover	Date Covered
Mon				
Tues				
Wed				
Thur				
Fri				

Specific concepts that still need to be reviewed/re-emphasized: _____
_____ Date Review Completed: __/__/20__

Day	Spelling and Handwriting	Quiz or Test	Main Concepts to Cover	Date Covered
Mon				
Tues				
Wed				
Thur				
Fri				

Specific concepts that still need to be reviewed/re-emphasized: _____
_____ Date Review Completed: __/__/20__

Day	Grammar and Phonics	Quiz or Test	Main Concepts to Cover	Date Covered
Mon				
Tues				
Wed				
Thur				
Fri				

Specific concepts that still need to be reviewed/re-emphasized: _____
_____ Date Review Completed: __/__/20__

Day	History	Quiz or Test	Main Concepts to Cover	Date Covered
Mon				
Tues				
Wed				
Thur				
Fri				

Specific concepts that still need to be reviewed/re-emphasized: _____

_____ Date Review Completed: __/__/20___

Day	Science	Quiz or Test	Main Concepts to Cover	Date Covered
Mon				
Tues				
Wed				
Thur				
Fri				

Specific concepts that still need to be reviewed/re-emphasized: _____

_____ Date Review Completed: __/__/20___

Day	Math	Quiz or Test	Main Concepts to Cover	Date Covered
Mon				
Tues				
Wed				
Thur				
Fri				

Specific concepts that still need to be reviewed/re-emphasized: _____

_____ Date Review Completed: __/__/20___

Day	Other: _____	Quiz or Test	Main Concepts to Cover	Date Covered
Mon				
Tues				
Wed				
Thur				
Fri				

Specific concepts that still need to be reviewed/re-emphasized: _____

_____ Date Review Completed: __/__/20___

General Comments: _____

_____

Student: _____ Grade: _____ Week Beginning: _____

Weekly Lesson Planner

Day	Bible	Quiz or Test	Main Concepts to Cover	Date Covered
Mon				
Tues				
Wed				
Thur				
Fri				

Specific concepts that still need to be reviewed/re-emphasized: _____

_____ Date Review Completed: __/ / 20__

Day	Reading	Quiz or Test	Main Concepts to Cover	Date Covered
Mon				
Tues				
Wed				
Thur				
Fri				

Specific concepts that still need to be reviewed/re-emphasized: _____

_____ Date Review Completed: __/ / 20__

Day	Spelling and Handwriting	Quiz or Test	Main Concepts to Cover	Date Covered
Mon				
Tues				
Wed				
Thur				
Fri				

Specific concepts that still need to be reviewed/re-emphasized: _____

_____ Date Review Completed: __/ / 20__

Day	Grammar and Phonics	Quiz or Test	Main Concepts to Cover	Date Covered
Mon				
Tues				
Wed				
Thur				
Fri				

Specific concepts that still need to be reviewed/re-emphasized: _____

_____ Date Review Completed: __/ / 20__

Day	History	Quiz or Test	Main Concepts to Cover	Date Covered
Mon				
Tues				
Wed				
Thur				
Fri				

Specific concepts that still need to be reviewed/re-emphasized: _____
_____ Date Review Completed: __/__/20___

Day	Science	Quiz or Test	Main Concepts to Cover	Date Covered
Mon				
Tues				
Wed				
Thur				
Fri				

Specific concepts that still need to be reviewed/re-emphasized: _____
_____ Date Review Completed: __/__/20___

Day	Math	Quiz or Test	Main Concepts to Cover	Date Covered
Mon				
Tues				
Wed				
Thur				
Fri				

Specific concepts that still need to be reviewed/re-emphasized: _____
_____ Date Review Completed: __/__/20___

Day	Other: _____	Quiz or Test	Main Concepts to Cover	Date Covered
Mon				
Tues				
Wed				
Thur				
Fri				

Specific concepts that still need to be reviewed/re-emphasized: _____
_____ Date Review Completed: __/__/20___

General Comments: _____
_____

Student: _____ Grade: _____ Week Beginning: _____

Weekly Lesson Planner

Day	Bible	Quiz or Test	Main Concepts to Cover	Date Covered
Mon				
Tues				
Wed				
Thur				
Fri				

Specific concepts that still need to be reviewed/re-emphasized: _____

_____ Date Review Completed: _/ / 20___

Day	Reading	Quiz or Test	Main Concepts to Cover	Date Covered
Mon				
Tues				
Wed				
Thur				
Fri				

Specific concepts that still need to be reviewed/re-emphasized: _____

_____ Date Review Completed: _/ / 20___

Day	Spelling and Handwriting	Quiz or Test	Main Concepts to Cover	Date Covered
Mon				
Tues				
Wed				
Thur				
Fri				

Specific concepts that still need to be reviewed/re-emphasized: _____

_____ Date Review Completed: _/ / 20___

Day	Grammar and Phonics	Quiz or Test	Main Concepts to Cover	Date Covered
Mon				
Tues				
Wed				
Thur				
Fri				

Specific concepts that still need to be reviewed/re-emphasized: _____

_____ Date Review Completed: _/ / 20___

Day	History	Quiz or Test	Main Concepts to Cover	Date Covered
Mon				
Tues				
Wed				
Thur				
Fri				

Specific concepts that still need to be reviewed/re-emphasized: _____
_____ Date Review Completed: __/__/20__

Day	Science	Quiz or Test	Main Concepts to Cover	Date Covered
Mon				
Tues				
Wed				
Thur				
Fri				

Specific concepts that still need to be reviewed/re-emphasized: _____
_____ Date Review Completed: __/__/20__

Day	Math	Quiz or Test	Main Concepts to Cover	Date Covered
Mon				
Tues				
Wed				
Thur				
Fri				

Specific concepts that still need to be reviewed/re-emphasized: _____
_____ Date Review Completed: __/__/20__

Day	Other: _____	Quiz or Test	Main Concepts to Cover	Date Covered
Mon				
Tues				
Wed				
Thur				
Fri				

Specific concepts that still need to be reviewed/re-emphasized: _____
_____ Date Review Completed: __/__/20__

General Comments: _____

_____

Student: _____ Grade: _____ Week Beginning: _____

Weekly Lesson Planner

Day	Bible	Quiz or Test	Main Concepts to Cover	Date Covered
Mon				
Tues				
Wed				
Thur				
Fri				

Specific concepts that still need to be reviewed/re-emphasized: _____
_____ Date Review Completed: _/ _/ 20 _

Day	Reading	Quiz or Test	Main Concepts to Cover	Date Covered
Mon				
Tues				
Wed				
Thur				
Fri				

Specific concepts that still need to be reviewed/re-emphasized: _____
_____ Date Review Completed: _/ _/ 20 _

Day	Spelling and Handwriting	Quiz or Test	Main Concepts to Cover	Date Covered
Mon				
Tues				
Wed				
Thur				
Fri				

Specific concepts that still need to be reviewed/re-emphasized: _____
_____ Date Review Completed: _/ _/ 20 _

Day	Grammar and Phonics	Quiz or Test	Main Concepts to Cover	Date Covered
Mon				
Tues				
Wed				
Thur				
Fri				

Specific concepts that still need to be reviewed/re-emphasized: _____
_____ Date Review Completed: _/ _/ 20 _

Day	History	Quiz or Test	Main Concepts to Cover	Date Covered
Mon				
Tues				
Wed				
Thur				
Fri				

Specific concepts that still need to be reviewed/re-emphasized: _____

_____ Date Review Completed: __/__/20__

Day	Science	Quiz or Test	Main Concepts to Cover	Date Covered
Mon				
Tues				
Wed				
Thur				
Fri				

Specific concepts that still need to be reviewed/re-emphasized: _____

_____ Date Review Completed: __/__/20__

Day	Math	Quiz or Test	Main Concepts to Cover	Date Covered
Mon				
Tues				
Wed				
Thur				
Fri				

Specific concepts that still need to be reviewed/re-emphasized: _____

_____ Date Review Completed: __/__/20__

Day	Other: _____	Quiz or Test	Main Concepts to Cover	Date Covered
Mon				
Tues				
Wed				
Thur				
Fri				

Specific concepts that still need to be reviewed/re-emphasized: _____

_____ Date Review Completed: __/__/20__

General Comments: _____

_____

Curriculum Listing

School Year 20___–20___

School Name: _____

Student's Name: _____   Grade Level: _____

Core Curriculum

Subjects	Title of Books or Educational Materials	Publishers
Bible		
Phonics		
Reading		
Handwriting		
Spelling		
Grammar		
Science		
Mathematics		
History		
Art		
Physical Education		
Music		

List of Supplemental/Enrichment Materials

Subjects	Title of Books/Educational Materials Used	Publishers

Student's Name: _____   Week Ending: _____

Assignment Record

Subject	Assignment	Due Date	Completed

General Comments: _____

_____

_____

Student's Name: _____   Week Ending: _____

Weekly Assignment Sheet

Days	Reading and Phonics
Mon	
Tues	
Wed	
Thur	
Fri	

Days	Penmanship
Mon	
Tues	
Wed	
Thur	
Fri	

Days	Mathematics
Mon	
Tues	
Wed	
Thur	
Fri	

Days	History
Mon	
Tues	
Wed	
Thur	
Fri	

Days	Government
Mon	
Tues	
Wed	
Thur	
Fri	

Days	Art & Music
Mon	
Tues	
Wed	
Thur	
Fri	

Days	Bible Studies
Mon	
Tues	
Wed	
Thur	
Fri	

Days	Physical Education
Mon	
Tues	
Wed	
Thur	
Fri	

Days	Grammar
Mon	
Tues	
Wed	
Thur	
Fri	

Days	Other
Mon	
Tues	
Wed	
Thur	
Fri	

Teacher's Comments: _____

_____

(Note: A weekly assignment sheet should be given to each student every Monday morning. The instructor can use this form to check his student's daily progress as well.)

Record of Materials Sent to CLASS to be Graded

Student's Name: _____   Student ID: _____

Grade Level: _____   School Year: _____   Family ID: _____

Subjects	Description of Items Sent (Test, Quiz, etc. Include Test # or Page #)	Sent Via		Date Sent
		UPS	USPS	

General Comments: _____

_____

_____

Reading Record Sheet

School Name: _____

Address: _____

City: _____ State: _____ Zip Code: _____

Student's Name: _____ **Grade Level:** _____

School Year 20___–20___   **Teacher's Name:** _____

1.	Category:	Date Started:
	Title:	Date Finished:
	Author:	Teacher's Initial:
2.	Category:	Date Started:
	Title:	Date Finished:
	Author:	Teacher's Initial:
3.	Category:	Date Started:
	Title:	Date Finished:
	Author:	Teacher's Initial:
4.	Category:	Date Started:
	Title:	Date Finished:
	Author:	Teacher's Initial:
5.	Category:	Date Started:
	Title:	Date Finished:
	Author:	Teacher's Initial:
6.	Category:	Date Started:
	Title:	Date Finished:
	Author:	Teacher's Initial:
7.	Category:	Date Started:
	Title:	Date Finished:
	Author:	Teacher's Initial:
8.	Category:	Date Started:
	Title:	Date Finished:
	Author:	Teacher's Initial:
9.	Category:	Date Started:
	Title:	Date Finished:
	Author:	Teacher's Initial:

10.	Category:	Date Started:
	Title:	Date Finished:
	Author:	Teacher's Initial:
11.	Category:	Date Started:
	Title:	Date Finished:
	Author:	Teacher's Initial:
12.	Category:	Date Started:
	Title:	Date Finished:
	Author:	Teacher's Initial:
13.	Category:	Date Started:
	Title:	Date Finished:
	Author:	Teacher's Initial:
14.	Category:	Date Started:
	Title:	Date Finished:
	Author:	Teacher's Initial:
15.	Category:	Date Started:
	Title:	Date Finished:
	Author:	Teacher's Initial:
16.	Category:	Date Started:
	Title:	Date Finished:
	Author:	Teacher's Initial:
17.	Category:	Date Started:
	Title:	Date Finished:
	Author:	Teacher's Initial:
18.	Category:	Date Started:
	Title:	Date Finished:
	Author:	Teacher's Initial:
19.	Category:	Date Started:
	Title:	Date Finished:
	Author:	Teacher's Initial:

Categories include:

Classical Novel	Short Story Anthology	Christian Fiction	Diaries and Journals
Historical Novel	Play Script	Christian Nonfiction	Devotional
Drama	Poetry	Modern Fiction	Research Paper Book
Political Affairs	Fiction	Scientific Fiction	Autobiography
Biography	Nonfiction	Scientific Nonfiction	Sermon

Attendance Record

School Name: _____

Address: _____

City: _____ State: _____ Zip Code: _____

Date School Year Began: _____ School Year: _____

Total Attendance Days: _____ Total Days Absent: _____

Student's Name: _____ Age: _____

Grade Level: _____ Sex: _____

Date School Year Ended: _____

Months	1	2	3	4	5	6	7	8	9	10	11	12	13	14	15	16	17	18	19	20	21	22	23	24	25	26	27	28	29	30	31
September																															
October																															
November																															
December																															
January																															
February																															
March																															
April																															
May																															
June																															
July																															
August																															

General Comments: _____

_____

_____

_____

School Name: _____

Address: _____

City: _____ State: _____ Zip Code: _____

Report Card

Student ID	Student's Name	Grade Level	Quarter	Qtr. Ending

Course Description		Test Number and Test Scores																				Grades			
		1	2	3	4	5	6	7	8	9	10	11	12	13	14	15	16	17	18	19	20	Qtr Test Avg	Test To Date	Daily Work Score	Final* Grade
	Qtr																								
	Score																								
	Qtr																								
	Score																								
	Qtr																								
	Score																								
	Qtr																								
	Score																								
	Qtr																								
	Score																								
	Qtr																								
	Score																								
	Qtr																								
	Score																								
	Qtr																								
	Score																								
	Qtr																								
	Score																								
	Qtr																								
	Score																								
	Qtr																								
	Score																								
	Qtr																								
	Score																								
	Qtr																								
	Score																								
	Qtr																								
	Score																								

This grade level was completed on _____

School Year 20___ –20___

Comments: _____

Grading Scale

1st Quarter ends–October 31	A = 100–94	S = Satisfactory
2nd Quarter ends–January 27	B = 93–87	U = Unsatisfactory
3rd Quarter ends–April 7	C = 86–77	
4th Quarter ends–June 16	D = 76–70	
	F = 69–0	

* Final Grade indicates course completed.

Student's Evaluation Report

Student's Name: _____ Grade Level: _____ School Year: 20___–20___

| 4–Excellent | 3–Good | 2–Satisfactory | 1–Needs Improvement |

Study Habits

	1st Qtr	2nd Qtr	3rd Qtr	4th Qtr
Makes good use of time				
Follows directions				
Works well independently				
Does not disturb others				
Does work neatly				
Takes care of educational materials				
Completes work required				
Reading speed (words per minute)				

Spiritual Development

	1st Qtr	2nd Qtr	3rd Qtr	4th Qtr
Reads Bible regularly				
Courteous to friends and strangers				
Gets along well with others in the family				
Exhibits self-control/government				
Shows respect for authority				
Responds well to correction				
Prays regularly for others				

Personal Development

	1st Qtr	2nd Qtr	3rd Qtr	4th Qtr
Ability to establish own goals				
Success in reaching objectives				
Flexibility				
Creativity				
Demonstrates perseverance				
General overall progress				

Teacher's Comments: _____

_____

Elementary Academic Record

Name: _____ Address: _____

School: _____ Home telephone: _____

Date of Birth: _____ Place of Birth: _____ Sex: _____

Father's Name: _____ Mother's Name: _____

Date Entered: _____ Former School: _____ Withdrawal Date: _____

Comments: _____

GRADE K	SCHOOL YEAR _____				
SUBJECTS	1	2	3	4	FINAL
Bible					
Phonics					
Handwriting					
Science					
Mathematics					
History					
Reading					

GRADE 4	SCHOOL YEAR _____				
SUBJECTS	1	2	3	4	FINAL
Bible					
Phonics					
Handwriting					
Science					
Mathematics					
History					
Reading					
Spelling					

GRADE 1	SCHOOL YEAR _____				
SUBJECTS	1	2	3	4	FINAL
Bible					
Phonics					
Handwriting					
Science					
Mathematics					
History					
Reading					
Spelling					

GRADE 5	SCHOOL YEAR _____				
SUBJECTS	1	2	3	4	FINAL
Bible					
Phonics					
Handwriting					
Science					
Mathematics					
History/Geography					
Reading					
Spelling					

GRADE 2	SCHOOL YEAR _____				
SUBJECTS	1	2	3	4	FINAL
Bible					
Phonics					
Handwriting					
Science					
Mathematics					
History					
Reading					
Spelling					

GRADE 6	SCHOOL YEAR _____				
SUBJECTS	1	2	3	4	FINAL
Bible					
Phonics					
Handwriting					
Science					
Mathematics					
History/Geography					
Reading					
Spelling					

GRADE 3	SCHOOL YEAR _____				
SUBJECTS	1	2	3	4	FINAL
Bible					
Phonics					
Handwriting					
Science					
Mathematics					
History					
Reading					
Spelling					

RETAINED	SCHOOL YEAR _____				
SUBJECTS	1	2	3	4	FINAL
Bible					
Phonics					
Handwriting					
Science					
Mathematics					
History					
Reading					
Spelling					

Junior High School Academic Record

Name: _____   Address: _____

School: _____   Home telephone: _____

Date of Birth: _____   Place of Birth: _____ Sex: ____

Father's Name: _____   Mother's Name: _____

Date Entered: _____   Former School: _____ Withdrawal Date: ____

Comments: _____

GRADE 7		SCHOOL YEAR _____				
SUBJECTS		1	2	3	4	FINAL
Bible						
Phonics						
Handwriting						
Science						
Mathematics						
History						
Reading						
Spelling						

GRADE ___		SCHOOL YEAR _____				
SUBJECTS		1	2	3	4	FINAL
Bible						
Phonics						
Handwriting						
Science						
Mathematics						
History						
Reading						
Spelling						

GRADE 8		SCHOOL YEAR _____				
SUBJECTS		1	2	3	4	FINAL
Bible						
Phonics						
Handwriting						
Science						
Mathematics						
History/Civics						
Reading						
Spelling						

GRADE ___		SCHOOL YEAR _____				
SUBJECTS		1	2	3	4	FINAL
Bible						
Phonics						
Handwriting						
Science						
Mathematics						
History						
Reading						
Spelling						

GRADE ___		SCHOOL YEAR _____				
SUBJECTS		1	2	3	4	FINAL
Bible						
Phonics						
Handwriting						
Science						
Mathematics						
History						
Reading						
Spelling						

GRADE ___		SCHOOL YEAR _____				
SUBJECTS		1	2	3	4	FINAL
Bible						
Phonics						
Handwriting						
Science						
Mathematics						
History						
Reading						
Spelling						

GRADE ___		SCHOOL YEAR _____				
SUBJECTS		1	2	3	4	FINAL
Bible						
Phonics						
Handwriting						
Science						
Mathematics						
History						
Reading						
Spelling						

GRADE ___		SCHOOL YEAR _____				
SUBJECTS		1	2	3	4	FINAL
Bible						
Phonics						
Handwriting						
Science						
Mathematics						
History						
Reading						
Spelling						

High School Curriculum Plan

Tentative Course of Study for High School

USE THIS FORM FOR A STUDENT
AT THE 9TH GRADE AND ABOVE.

Date: _____

Name: _____

General College or Career Plans: _____
_____
_____
_____
_____
_____

NOTE TO PARENTS/TEACHERS:

When your student is chronologically of high school age it is time to consider graduation goals, career potential, and God's calling for the child. Listed on the reverse side are the required and elective courses for students enrolled in the Christian Liberty Academy. This information will serve as a guide to you in making up the graduation goals for each student. You will need to modify your graduation program for each child to fit his goals and potential. Remember, the key is to outline a course of study that will give each student the maximum amount of academic/career options after graduation.

9th Grade – School Year

Subject	1 Qtr	2 Qtr	Cr	3 Qtr	4 Qtr	Cr
Bible						
Language Arts						
Mathematics						
Science						
Government/Civics						
Literature						
World History						
American History						
Foreign Language						
Economics						

10th Grade – School Year

	1 Qtr	2 Qtr	Cr	3 Qtr	4 Qtr	Cr

11th Grade – School Year _____

Subject	1 Qtr	2 Qtr	Cr	3 Qtr	4 Qtr	Cr
Bible						
Language Arts						
Mathematics						
Science						
Government/Civics						
Literature						
World History						
American History						
Foreign Language						
Economics						

12th Grade – School Year _____

	1 Qtr	2 Qtr	Cr	3 Qtr	4 Qtr	Cr

Comments: _____
_____

Student's Signature: _____ Date: _____

Teacher's Signature: _____ Date: _____

Suggested Courses To Obtain a High School Diploma

1. Four credits of Bible (including at least 1 credit of Old Testament studies and 1 credit of New Testament studies)

2. Four credits of English (including at least 1 credit of grammar, 1/2 credit of composition, and 1 credit of literature)

3. Seven credits of social studies (including at least 1 credit of US history, 1 credit of world history, 1 credit of economics, and 1 credit of governemnt)

4. Two credits of science (including at least 1 credit of biology)

5. Two credits of math (including at least 1 credit of Algebra I or higher level course)

Suggested Elective Choices

Mathematics	Science	Social Studies	English
Algebra II*	Physical Science	Church History	Creative Writing
Geometry*	General Science	Geography	Speech
Trigonometry	Chemistry*	US Constitution	
Calculus	Physics		
Business Math			

Foreign Language*	Vocational Studies	Bible
German I and II	Sewing	Advanced Theology
Latin I and II	Cooking	Family Life
French I and II	Typing	Philosophy
Spanish I and II	Computer	
	Woodworking	
	Accounting	

*Recommended for college entrance

An academic course load will usually consist of four to seven courses per year, depending upon the student's abilities and interests. It may be wise to contact several prospective colleges to obtain detailed information regarding their specific entrance requirements so you can be sure to assign the necessary courses for college entrance. Check your local state requirements as well.

High School Transcript Record

School Name: _____   Student's Name: _____

Addresss: _____   Date Issued: _____ Issued by: _____

_____   Total Credits: _____

Subjects	Grade					Subjects	Grade			
	9	10	11	12			9	10	11	12
Bible, Theology						U.S. History				
Philosophy						World History				
Spelling						Church History				
Speech, Writing						Government/Civics				
English						Economics				
General Math						Geography				
Algebra I, II						French, Spanish				
Geometry, Trigonometry						Latin, German				
Calculus, Business Math						Physical Education				
General Science						Art				
Earth, Physical Science						Music				
Biology, Physics, Chemistry										

1/2 = 1/2 Credit   U = Unsatisfactory   * = No academic credit given

S = Satisfactory   I = Incomplete   G = Grade to date; course incomplete

High School Graduation Standing		Grading Scale	
G.P.A.: _____ Total Possible: _____		A = 94-100	B = 87 - 93
		C = 77 - 86	D = 70 - 76

Comments: _____

_____

Student's Signature: _____ Date: _____

Teacher's Signature: _____ Date: _____

Academic Transcript Report

School Name: _____

Address: _____

City: _____ State _____ Zip Code: _____

Student's Name: _____ Grade Level: _____ School Year: 20___ –20___

School Year: 20___ –20___   Issued by: _____

Grading Scale	A = 94 - 100	B = 87 - 93	C = 77 - 86	D = 70 - 76

Subjects	Textbook Publisher	1st Qtr	2nd Qtr	3rd Qtr	4th Qtr	Final
Bible						
English/Grammar						
Literature						
Spelling						
Phonics						
History						
Economics						
Government						
Constitution						
Geography						
Science						
Math						
Reading						
Penmanship						
Church History						
Philosophy						
Foreign Language						
Home Economics						
Physical Education						
Art						
Music						

Teacher's Comments: _____

Disciplinary Action Record

Nature of Incident: _____ Date: _____

Action Taken: _____

Results of Discipline: _____

Achievement Test Results

Test Name: _____ Form: _____ Date of Testing: _____

Areas Tested		Score	G.E.	Areas Tested		Score	G.E.
Reading	Vocabulary			Language	Auding		
	Comprehension				Mechanics		
Mathematics	Computation				Usage & Structure		
	Concepts				Spelling		

Total Battery: _____

Project

Worksheet Schedule

Student's Name: _____

Grade Level: _____ School Year: _____

Proj #	Name of Projects	Activities	Schedule Date		Actual Date		Teacher
			Start	Finish	Start	Finish	Initial
1.							
2.							
3.							
4.							
5.							
6.							
7.							
8.							
9.							
10.							
11.							
12.							
13.							
14.							
15.							
16.							
17.							
18.							

Field Trip

**Worksheet
Schedule**

Student's Name: _____

Grade Level: _____ School Year: _____

Date Scheduled	Number of Students	Location of Field Trip	Activities Planned	Completed Field Trip

Comments: _____

_____ Date: _____

Comments: _____

_____ Date: _____

Comments: _____

_____ Date: _____

TODAY

Appointment		Things to do today	Call	Done
6:30				
7:00				
7:30				
8:00				
8:30				
9:00				
9:30				
10:00				
10:30				
11:00				
11:30				
12:00				
12:30				
1:00				
1:30				
2:00				
2:30				
3:00				
3:30				
4:00				
4:30				
5:00				
5:30				
6:00				
6:30				
7:00				
7:30				
8:00				
8:30				

Notes: _____

_____

_____

_____

Weekly Chore List

Student's Name: _____   Week Ending: _____

Days	Kitchen Chores	Laundry Chores	General Household	Other Chores
Mon	Do the dishes, clean counters, stove, etc. Completed ☐	Completed ☐	Completed ☐	Completed ☐
Tues	Do the dishes, clean counters, stove, etc. Completed ☐	Sort & wash, fold & put away clothes (if necessary) Completed ☐	Vacuum floors Completed ☐	Completed ☐
Wed	Do the dishes, clean counters, stove, etc.; dust & mop floor Completed ☐	Iron and put away clothes Completed ☐	Completed ☐	Organize own bedroom Completed ☐
Thurs	Do the dishes, clean counters, sink, etc. Completed ☐	Completed ☐	Vacuum floors Completed ☐	Completed ☐
Fri	Do the dishes, clean counters, stove, etc. Completed ☐	Completed ☐	Completed ☐	Completed ☐
Sat	Do the dishes, clean counters, stove, etc.; dust & mop floor Completed ☐	Clean up the laundry room/area; wash, fold & put away clothes Completed ☐	Dust house; clean mirrors, windows,; do bathroom(s); vacuum Completed ☐	Organize own bedroom Completed ☐

Whenever possible, divide up the chores among all members of the household. In this way, each family member will be responsible for certain duties that will take only a few minutes each day. In the empty squares, you may also include other household chores that you deem necessary. The *Other Chores* category is provided to remind students to take responsibility for the cleaning and organizing of their own belongings.

Some families set aside one day each week, perhaps Saturday, for the cleaning duties above. However, this approach may be adapted for your family's needs.

Have your student(s) put a check mark (✔) in the square as soon as a chore is completed.

"Let all things be done decently and in order." 1 Corinthians 14:40

VACATION SCHEDULE

NAME		JAN.	FEB.	MAR.	APR.	MAY	JUNE	JULY	AUG.	SEPT.	OCT.	NOV.	DEC.
	Week 1												
	Week 2												
	Week 3												
	Week 4												
	Week 5												
	Week 1												
	Week 2												
	Week 3												
	Week 4												
	Week 5												
	Week 1												
	Week 2												
	Week 3												
	Week 4												
	Week 5												
	Week 1												
	Week 2												
	Week 3												
	Week 4												
	Week 5												
	Week 1												
	Week 2												
	Week 3												
	Week 4												
	Week 5												
	Week 1												
	Week 2												
	Week 3												
	Week 4												
	Week 5												
	Week 1												
	Week 2												
	Week 3												
	Week 4												
	Week 5												
	Week 1												
	Week 2												
	Week 3												
	Week 4												
	Week 5												
	Week 1												
	Week 2												
	Week 3												
	Week 4												
	Week 5												
	Week 1												
	Week 2												
	Week 3												
	Week 4												
	Week 5												
	Week 1												
	Week 2												
	Week 3												
	Week 4												
	Week 5												

Fill in appropriate weeks. Use 5th week where applicable.

Month Organizer

S	M	T	W	T	F	S

Physician's Health Report

Student's Name: _____ Birthdate: _____

Weight: _____ Height: _____ Sex: _____ M _____ F _____

Medical History	Age at onset	Immunizations	Date Given	Physical Exam	Date Given
Asthma		d.p.t. 1		Eyes	
Chicken Pox		d.p.t. 2		Skin and Hair	
Convulsions		d.p.t. 3		Ears	
Diabetes		d.p.t. 4		Nose and Throat	
Diphtheria		dt		Mouth and Teeth	
Discharging Ears		Polio 1		Coordination	
Heart Disease		Polio 2		Chest	
Measles:		Polio 3		Heart	
Type		Booster		Abdomen	
Type		Rubella Vaccine		Genitalia	
Type		Tetanus		Hernia	
Mumps		Measles		Skeletal	
Polio		Recommendations for Physical Activities		Recommendations for care of this student	
Pneumonia					
Rheumatic Fever					
Scarlet Fever					
Whooping Cough					
Other					
Other					
Other					

Is the student now under treatment for any medical or emotional disorder? If so, please specify.

_____

_____

_____   _____   _____
Parent/Guardian Signature   *Physician's Signature*   *Date of Examination*

Parent/Guardian:	Physician's Name:
Address:	Address:
City, State, Zip Code:	City, State, Zip Code:
Phone #:	Phone #:

Health Examination Certificate

Name: _____ Birthdate: _____

Age: _____ Sex: _____ Weight: _____ Height: _____ Blood Pressure: _____

Skin: _____

Vision: Without Glasses: R: 20/_____ L: 20/_____ With Glasses: R: 20/_____ L: 20/_____

Hearing: _____

_____

Mouth, Nose, Throat: _____

_____

Heart and Lungs: _____

_____

Tuberculosis: _____

_____

Immunization: _____

_____

Abdomen: _____

_____

Genito-Urinary: _____

_____

Nervous and Mental: _____

_____

Additional Findings: _____

_____

Recommendations: _____

_____

This is to certify that an examination of the above-named person shows the results indicated, and that he/she is ____ is not ____ free of tuberculosis or other communicable disease, or any disease, physical or mental, which will impair the ability of this person to attend school.

Physician's Signature: _____ Date: _____

Prayer Journal

Things to Pray for:	Date Requested	Date Answered
Prayers of Thanksgiving or Praise		
1.		
2.		
3.		
Family Members (list specific prayer needs)		
1.		
2.		
3.		
4.		
5.		
Prayer for Christian Missions		
1.		
2.		
3.		
Prayer for Civil Leaders or Civil Elections		
1.		
2.		
3.		
Prayer for Church Leaders or Church Programs		
1.		
2.		
3.		
Special Prayer Requests		
1.		
2.		
3.		

"Be careful for nothing; but in everything by prayer and supplication with thanksgiving let your requests be made known unto God." Philippians 4:6

Outstanding Achievement
Award

Presented to:

for
Exceptional Work in

During the Week of

Train up a child in the
way he should go, and
when he is old, he will not
depart from it.

Proverbs 22:6

Teacher's Signature

Outstanding Achievement
Award

Presented to:

for
Exceptional Work in

During the Week of

Train up a child in the
way he should go, and
when he is old, he will not
depart from it.

Proverbs 22:6

Teacher's Signature